If I Had Only Known

Checklists And Guidance
Before And After A Loved One Dies

JENNIFER A. BORISLOW
MELISSA A. MARRAMA
MICHAELA F. SCOTT

Strategic Vision Publishing

Disclaimer

This publication does not attempt to illustrate the precise legal, tax, accounting, or investment consequences of a particular situation. The precise consequences of a particular situation depend on many variables, some of which may not be accounted for or fully described in this publication.

You should consult your own legal and tax advisors before you make any estate or business planning decisions (or change title to any assets or beneficiary designations) to determine (1) the suitability of a particular solution, and (2) the precise legal, tax, investment, and accounting consequences of that decision. We do not give legal, tax, or accounting advice. We assume no liability for the use of the information contained in this guidebook. You assume responsibility for your financial decisions. It is important to revise your strategies periodically in light of your experiences and changing goals.

Strategic Vision Publishing, LLC
1 Griffin Brook Drive
Methuen, MA 01844

Printed in the United States of America

ISBN 978-0-9825459-5-9

For more information on Jennifer A. Borislow, Melissa A. Marrama, or Michaela F. Scott, email info@strategicvisionpublishing.com

Copies of this book may be purchased for educational, business, or promotional use. Please contact orders@strategicvisionpublishing.com.

Dedication

This book is dedicated to our families, friends, and fellow advisors, who have championed our passion to help people define and secure their legacies for those they love. We also dedicate this book to our wonderful clients, who have placed their trust in us over the past 36 years: Each experience of yours has uniquely contributed to the creation of this guidebook. We are honored to be part of your team and humbled to be counted among the people you confide in during the most difficult times of your lives.

CONTENTS

Foreword / 1

Introduction / 3

Part One: Planning Your Legacy / 5

- **Before You Get Started /** 6
- **When Should You Plan Your Estate? /** 6

Section I: Trusted Advisors: Your People / 11

- **Who Are Your People? /** 12
- **The Inner Circle:The People Who Help You Decide What to Do /** 12
- **The Professionals: People Whose Advice, Insights, and Services You Rely on to Plan and Execute Your Final Wishes /** 14
- **Your People /** 18

Section II: Inventory: Your Assets and Your Obligations / 19

- **Where Is It? /** 20
- **Asset Inventory and Location /** 22
- **Asset Ownership and Beneficiaries /** 24
- **Beneficiary/Owner Inventory /** 28
- **Digital Assets /** 30
- **Digital Asset Inventory /** 31
- **Planning Ahead: Your Facebook Account /** 32
- **Planning Ahead: Your Google Account /** 34
- **Planning Ahead: Your Twitter Account /** 34
- **Planning Ahead: Your Instagram Account /** 35

Section III: Estate Planning / 37

- **Choose Your Legacy** / 38
- **Legal Documents** / 39
- **If You Become Unable to Make Your Own Decisions** / 39
- **Healthcare Power of Attorney** / 45
- **Power of Attorney and Financial Decisions** / 46
- **The Value of Wills** / 47
- **The Value of Trusts** / 53
- **Important Issues to Raise About Legal Documents** / 59
- **Estate Planning Items for Discussion** / 62
- **Tax Planning** / 65
- **Keep the IRS Happy** / 65
- **Financial Planning** / 68
- **Charitable Giving** / 76
- **Life Changes** / 79
- **Titling and Beneficiaries** / 79

Section IV: Personal Wishes / 81

- **Take the Pressure Off Your Loved Ones** / 82
- **Funeral Planning** / 82
- **Funeral Planning** / 84
- **Other Important Expressions of Your Wishes** / 90
- **If Death Is Imminent** / 92
- **The Greatest Gift You Give** / 93

Part Two: After a Loved One Has Died / 95

- **Gaining Confidence: Caring for Yourself and Others … and Upholding Your Loved One's Wishes** / 96
- **Immediate Action Steps** / 97
- **Funeral Arrangements** / 101

- **About the Death Certificate** / 103
- **In the Days Following a Loved One's Passing** / 106
- **Organizing Your Team and Identifying Responsibilities** / 109
- **Different Situations, Different Levels of Discovery** / 111
- **The Executor** / 112
- **Learn from the Experience of Others!** / 114
- **Officially Becoming the Executor** / 119
- **Bank Accounts and Bills** / 121
- **People to Notify** / 123
- **Death Claims, Retitling Assets, and Related Issues** / 126
- **Distributing Assets** / 127
- **Identity Theft** / 128
- **Closing Thoughts** / 133

Worksheets / 135

About the Authors / 149

FOREWORD

At the age of 66, my father was diagnosed with lung and bladder cancer. He had retired just two years earlier after a successful 38-year career with Liberty Mutual Insurance, and we all thought my parents would finally have time to travel to all the fun destinations they had always dreamed of visiting. Those dreams were shattered by my father's cancer diagnosis.

I was extraordinarily close to my father. I am the firstborn child, I attended the same prep school he did, I served on several non-profit boards that he had served on, we worked in the same industry, and we shared many professional, personal, and career passions. In essence, I am a "chip off the old block."

When I learned of his diagnosis, I chose to be present every day to support him through his illness. There was a growing intimacy between us, and we both knew this journey would be a difficult one, a journey whose ending we could not predict. We were hopeful for a full recovery.

Given our similarities and closeness, it was no surprise that my father and I spent even more time together near the end of his life. What inspired me was how focused and purposeful this final period of his life turned out to be.

My father prepared our family for his passing. He was a planner; he knew he had a job to do and was focused on getting it done. That job was to make sure my mother would be well taken care of and would never have to worry about her financial security after he was gone. He was steadfast and committed to leaving his personal and financial affairs in order, and he relied on me to help him complete that job. He was diligent and thorough, and his final months were filled with great purpose.

As his illness progressed, my father and I spent more and more time talking about his legacy. The word "legacy" means different things to different people, but in the broadest sense its meaning is pretty clear—what one leaves behind. As he talked about his legacy, my father encouraged me to listen, take careful notes, and execute on his final wishes. He shared in detail what he wanted to happen and planned everything for the funeral service, from who would speak to what music would be played. He focused on putting his financial affairs in order and shared with his adult children how we could best emotionally support our mother after his death.

It took courage, patience, and discipline for him to have these planning discussions at the end of his life. He loved his family deeply and remained committed to helping all of us transition to the next phase of our lives. I will never forget the sense of responsibility, respect, and unconditional love I experienced, knowing that I could help him to finalize, record, and execute on his final wishes. Helping him prepare for death was a life-changing experience for me.

My father died peacefully on November 25, 2008. It was achingly hard to lose him, but that loss was tempered by our feelings of deep gratitude for the great gift he had left us: the gift of certainty about what would happen next. There were no missed deadlines, no hurt feelings, no last-minute emergencies, and no unexpected administrative problems for the family to deal with in the days after my father's passing. My mother made a good transition out of the initial period of grief and moved into the next phase of her life. As someone with deep experience in the insurance industry, I knew just how rare that was.

I started thinking more and more about the fact that most families are not as fortunate as ours had been. Most people who lose a loved one do not know what to do next.

My father's passing gave me a sense of deep purpose. From that experience, our amazing team at Borislow Insurance became even more passionate and committed to helping families have the kind of well-planned, well-executed experience that I was fortunate to have had. This book is a continuation of my father's legacy.

– Jennifer A. Borislow

INTRODUCTION

No one likes to think or talk about death and dying. It is not a happy subject. Nevertheless, the reality is that each of us will have to deal with the passing of a loved one and, sooner or later, will have to prepare for our own passing. Love never dies, but death is a natural part of life, and we must find a way to share our wishes with those we love.

A culmination of experiences, both personal and professional, inspired us to write this guidebook. As professionals who have helped numerous clients plan for and process the intimate details of a loved one's passing, we are passionate about our WHY—helping families—and we feel compelled to share what we know.

- We have witnessed first-hand the disorienting and emotionally devastating effects common planning oversights have on loved ones. The unexpected need to make urgent, time-sensitive decisions while still in shock over a loss can be overwhelming.

- We have heard too many people say, "If I only knew …" or "If he/she had only known …" in response to a needless disagreement over money or property that could easily have been avoided with just a little advice and expertise.

- We have navigated numerous client situations and have given precise directions for overcoming major challenges, so we feel a professional responsibility to share our knowledge on how to avoid the most common mistakes. More importantly, we are passionate about motivating and helping people make sense of the task of leaving their loved ones the invaluable gift of an organized estate with clearly communicated wishes.

- Each of us has had personal experiences with our own loved ones who inadvertently overlooked something important.

- We believe that we have a similar obligation to help people who find themselves responsible for settling an estate, particularly one in which there are unresolved issues.

- We know that when people have the right advisor, a personal desire to settle the important issues, and appropriate resources to "get their affairs in order," they are more likely to act.

For these reasons, we committed ourselves to the task of compiling and publishing several essential checklists and important tasks for families facing the death of a loved one. Our goal is to help educate and inspire people about why and how to begin taking action both before death and after losing a loved one.

Each family's situation is unique, and there are countless variations on even the most common scenarios. This can make taking that first step seem overwhelming. We have made a special effort to highlight the simplest and most important action items that will serve as a starting point and sustain your momentum. Getting started is crucial, because when it comes to planning and settling an estate, it is important to understand that *inaction is a choice*. In fact, it is often an extremely expensive choice—one that takes a heavy emotional and financial toll on those left behind.

Part One:
Planning Your Legacy

Before You Get Started

The first half of this guidebook is all about preparation *before* death occurs. You can benefit from this information whether you are planning your own estate or helping a loved one make these decisions.

If you are organizing and planning your final wishes on your own, it is important that you communicate your choices to at least one other person. Your final wishes must be known and understood if they are to be properly executed.

As you move through this guidebook, remember that sound estate planning is a precious gift that each of us can and should give our loved ones. Our aim is to help you make that gift possible. With the right team supporting you, you will find that one of the most difficult periods of life can become much more manageable—and your legacy will be something loved ones and family members will remember positively for decades to come.

Why You Should Plan

"The tragedy of failing to properly plan is not visited upon the dead. It is the living that suffer its unexpected and unforgiving consequences. By failing to properly plan, many of us are creating problems for our loved ones that would not otherwise exist. Estate planning sounds as if it is for the über-wealthy, when in fact it applies to everyone."

John J. Scroggin, *Estate Planning: It's All About Your Legacy*

When Should You Plan Your Estate?

Many people assume that the task of planning their estate should emerge as a priority later in life—when they are in their 50s or 60s—and certainly not when they are only in their 30s and 40s. It is common for this timing to be expressed not as a choice, but as an assumption: "I never really thought about it before. After all, I've got plenty of time, don't I?" If that is your mind-set let us respectfully suggest that you closely consider the following true story as a reminder that life is a precious gift and that you never know what tomorrow may bring.

Nicole and Jack were a happy, fun-loving couple who had lived together for several years and planned to get married. Both of them were in their early 30s, vibrant, in great health, with lots of friends and always on the go. Both loved their work and were dedicated to building their careers. They were enjoying life to its fullest and neither had taken any time to consider what would happen to them or their families in the event of a serious accident or illness. That kind of planning simply was not on their radar.

While on vacation in Florida, Nicole and Jack went out for a ride on a moped; Jack drove and Nicole rode behind him. It had rained earlier that evening, and the roads were still wet. On a poorly lit road, Jack made the mistake of hitting the accelerator a little too hard, and then had to brake sharply to try to make a tight turn that he had not seen coming. He lost control of the moped, ran a stop sign, and spun into an intersection. An oncoming tractor trailer hit them. Nicole was killed instantly, and Jack sustained major injuries from which he would never fully recover.

Nicole's parents, Tim and Barbara, got the dreaded phone call with the grim news that their young, active, energetic daughter had suddenly been killed, but that was only the beginning of a long nightmare. In shock and overcome with grief, they were faced with many logistical concerns that needed to be handled immediately.

Nicole was only 34 years old and had left no instructions on how to handle her funeral arrangements and final affairs. She also had no insurance policy in place to cover funeral expenses. In addition to processing the monumental grief that accompanies losing a child, Nicole's parents had to deal with the significant administrative, legal, and financial realities connected with making long-distance funeral arrangements. Think for just a moment about how difficult that must have been for them, and how emotionally unprepared they were to deal with that burden.

They did not have to fly to Florida to identify the body. Nicole's boyfriend was able, although just barely, to take that responsibility. They had no idea what kind of service, if any, Nicole would have wanted so they took advice from others that cremation was the most expeditious and inexpensive way to get the body home. In the absence of any instructions to the contrary, they arranged to have their daughter's body cremated and were surprised to discover that only the US Postal Service could transport the ashes to Massachusetts for the funeral service. They did the best they could under extremely trying circumstances. Unfortunately, their ordeal was not even close to over.

Nicole owned a small business and had a complex personal financial situation. She had multiple bank accounts, student loans, a car loan, and an outstanding business loan, in addition to several credit cards with balances. She paid all her bills online and the family did not know any of her account numbers or have access to any of her login information. Nicole left no clear instructions about any of her financial matters, and it was up to Tim and Barbara to sort everything out. They began by reviewing her incoming physical mail, talking to her friends, and convincing the landlord to allow them access to her apartment. They had no idea how to check her email, how to access any of her important accounts, or how to reach her accountant. All they had was the daily mail delivery. They spent countless hours on the phone trying to track down information, requesting forms, and looking up various contact numbers. In the search, they uncovered their obligation to pay the student loans as co-signers.

Nicole left no will—writing one was something she thought she could easily postpone until later in life. Tim and Barbara faced the monumental task of figuring out precisely what assets she had and how to distribute them.

Nicole's parents also had to face the sensitive question of what to do about Jack, who needed major medical care following the accident. Although Jack and Nicole were not married, he was covered under her health insurance plan as a domestic partner and had minimal health coverage on his own. Did Tim and Barbara have any moral or financial responsibility for his care?

One full year after Nicole's passing, Barbara and Tim are still dealing with unresolved issues. The number of administrative tasks has compounded their grief and left them with more questions than answers. It has delayed their healing process because they still do not have closure on their daughter's personal affairs.

We cannot ask Nicole this question, but we can ask you: *What would Nicole have wanted? Did she want her parents to make decisions for her? Did she want the burden of handling her affairs to rest solely on her grieving parents?*

The outcome would have been very different if Nicole had only known …

The lesson learned: If Nicole had thoughtfully planned, her parents or her boyfriend would have known exactly what to do and who the right people were to contact to execute on her wishes. They would have known who her accountant was, where she banked, and which loans or credit cards might have been on an automatic payment schedule. But she did not plan. As a result, her story is tragic and her life affairs, even a year after her passing, are complicated, burdensome, and messy for those who were closest to her.

Nicole's prolonged estate finalization, and her loved ones' lack of closure is, unfortunately, not unique. An adult child who dies with no clear direction leaves all responsibilities to their parents and loved ones. Advance planning is critically important, yet most people do not know where to start. That is why we have prepared some thought-provoking steps to help you get started:

- ☐ **Ask yourself, "Who would be most affected if something were to happen to me tomorrow—and what would that person have to do?"** This is not an easy subject to contemplate, but it is imperative that you ask the question and consider the consequences. Make a written list of the individuals who would be most immediately and adversely affected by your passing or your incapacitation—not just emotionally, but also logistically and financially—and then make some notes as to *how* each person would have to respond if something were to happen to you. Your list should specifically include the following information: Who will likely find themselves responsible for handling your funeral and/or memorial arrangements? How will that person know what your final wishes are? How will the funeral and/or memorial expenses be paid? Who will be responsible for settling your financial affairs? What kind of records will that person have access to? In the weeks or months following your incapacitation or passing, how easy or difficult will it be for that person to interact with your employer? Who are your insurance providers? Do you have any creditors? Who will be responsible for taking care of your loved ones—your children, aging parents, or pets? Who will tend to your household?

☐ **Put that list away and give yourself a few days before you look at it again.** Once you have had a little time to digest this difficult task, *review the list again closely.* Make any additions or changes you feel are necessary.

☐ **Now, set time aside for planning.** Creating and revising the list and considering the consequences will provide clarity on how important it is for you to take action. Clarity will lead to confidence in taking action to protect the security and peace of mind of those you love if something happens to you. Schedule uninterrupted time each week that you will devote to completing the items in this guidebook. Regardless of your age, it will benefit you greatly. It is important that you not only start the process, but also that you also follow through and finish it.

We know that there will be more questions than answers, so the next four sections are designed to help bring clarity and give you the tools and resources you need to complete the most important work you may ever do—specifying your personal wishes so you can leave your loved ones with peace of mind.

If you are reading this guidebook with pen or pencil in hand, we hope you feel empowered and accomplished with each new box you check and note you make during your planning sessions.

Now that you are in the mind-set of identifying your legacy and have started the process of planning, you are on your way!

Section I:
Trusted Advisors: Your People

Who Are Your People?

Dianne was the founder and CEO of a major fashion line. When she died at the age of 43, her business partner Lee was understandably grief-stricken. What Lee did not realize was that the grieving process was just the beginning of his troubles.

Dianne had provided generously for Lee in her will, yet she had not given Lee a copy of that will and had not shared with him information about the attorney and accountant who would be handling her estate. It took Lee weeks of stressful research to track down this important information. Dianne could have spared him much stress and anguish if she had prepared and shared a list of key contacts.

Which brings us to the question: Who are your people?

This part of the book will help you answer that important question. You should assemble a written master list with complete contact information of key people and update it annually. These people will fall into two separate groups.

The Inner Circle: The People Who Help You Decide What to Do

These are the people who will help you set priorities and get your affairs in order while there is still time to do so, and who will be there to help carry out your wishes once you are gone. These are the people you trust because they know you and they understand your intentions.

Here is a sampling of the kinds of people who should be in your inner circle and on this list. Note that some of these individuals may overlap, and that some categories (such as business partners) may not be relevant to your situation.

- *Guardian*: The person or people who will care for your minor children if you cannot. You should also identify at least two backup people in case the person you selected is unable to accept the responsibility at that time.

- *Healthcare Proxy*: The person who will make medical

decisions on your behalf if you cannot. You should also name at least two subsequent successors who can make decisions on your behalf if your first choice is not available.

- *Executor/Trustee*: The person or people who will be responsible for your estate after you die and will make sure what you have worked to build goes to the right beneficiaries as efficiently as possible. Again, name at least two additional backup people in case the person you selected is unable to accept the responsibility.

- *Durable Power of Attorney*: The person who will make financial decisions on your behalf if you are unable to. Name at least two backup choices.

- The loved ones you currently involve in major decisions.

- The business partners or co-workers your loved ones should connect with.

- Your employer.

- Your medical professionals: doctor(s), dentist, therapist(s), pharmacist.

- Any other important people (such as attorneys, accountants, clergy) who may already be part of your inner circle.

☐ **Identify and inform the specific people you have chosen to ensure that your final wishes are carried out.** Clearly identify the specific person (or persons) you feel most comfortable asking to execute your final wishes. This might be an adult child or family member, for instance, or it might be a trusted family friend. Avoid surprising anyone by assigning them a responsibility they might not expect. Take the time to make sure this person knows exactly what they are responsible for and is ready, willing, and able to carry out those responsibilities when the time comes. The duties in question may include implementing advance healthcare directives and working with your attorney to identify and communicate with the executor of your will.

The Professionals: People Whose Advice, Insights, and Services You Rely on to Plan and Execute Your Final Wishes

You may also choose to identify a team of professionals—individuals with the professional experience necessary to help assist you on the best way to address the most complex issues of your pre-death planning.

Estate planning involves many disciplines, and you may need help from professionals who are skilled in the areas of wills, trusts, insurance, bookkeeping and accounting, business planning, and the tax implications of gifts and bequests. You are not likely to find one individual who can handle all these areas. Based on your personal situation, the complexity of your assets, and your goals, you may decide that it makes sense to assemble a professional estate planning team.

Below, you will find a brief summary of the various roles of a professional estate planning team. Not all the professional roles will necessarily be relevant to your situation.

- *Estate Planning Attorney:* Based on the complexity of your asset holdings, you may decide that it makes sense to work with a licensed attorney who specializes in estate planning. This is an extremely important decision. If you opt to secure the services of an attorney for your estate planning, make sure you select an attorney who has sufficient expertise in estate, tax, and legal planning in the states in which you live and own property or businesses. Do your research, ask your professional advisors for referrals, and check references. Don't simply choose the least expensive attorney or someone who just happens to be your friend. Remember the adage: *You get what you pay for.* This is not an area where you want to spend less and get the wrong advice, particularly if you have a complex estate. If you decide to work with an attorney, be certain that you secure the services of a legal advisor or firm with deep experience and expertise to address your unique concerns.

- ***Tax Professional:*** Verify that you have the right Certified Public Accountant (CPA) working on your behalf. Do not automatically assume that the CPA firm you currently use to prepare your annual tax return is the right firm to assist with your estate planning. Just as you did with the attorney, you want to select someone with appropriate experience who can help you avoid costly mistakes. Choose a CPA and/or firm that is familiar with probate and estate tax issues in your state and the states where you have properties or business. Take the time to research—ask people you trust or other advisors for referrals, and then go and meet the people they recommend. Make sure the firm can handle multiple properties in multiple states, if that is your situation. If the CPA you are working with is not familiar with the state(s) in question, you will end up having to deal with multiple accountants, potential communication challenges, and increased margin for error.

- ***Financial Advisor:*** It is possible that one of the listed professionals on your team has special training in comprehensive financial planning and can take more than one role, and perhaps can even serve as your team's financial "quarterback". Alternatively, a single professional who specializes in financial planning may be part of your team. In either case, this person will likely take an active role in the formation and regular review of the overall estate plan, coordinating with the other members of your team.

- ***Insurance Professional:*** It is important to include an insurance advisor on your team of experts. You will want to meet regularly to review your existing insurance coverage and to revise the policies as necessary based on current goals. Postponing this kind of review can lead to unnecessary problems. It is important to work on an ongoing basis with a professional insurance advisor who has a deep knowledge and expertise with estate planning issues. Select an advisor who has the resources and necessary independence to approach questions without bias—someone you trust to sit on your side of the table.

- **Investment Advisor:** This is someone who helps you manage your investment portfolio and provides an overview of your retirement assets. This person can help you understand your retirement goals and project long-term retirement success in addition to how much money you may leave behind if you pass away at or beyond life expectancy. This person can also help you identify the financial options that support your estate planning goals.

- **Planned Giving Specialist:** If there is a particular charitable organization you want to support with a gift or bequest, reach out to them now. They may have an expert who can help you maximize any future gifts and bequests.

- **Trust Administrator:** If you select a bank or trust company as executor or co-executor of your will or trustee of your trust, you may choose to work with a trust administrator employed by that institution to help you plan and administer the estate.

- **Appraiser:** This person can help you determine the current value of your property. Why would you consider paying for that? Well, if you were running a yard sale, would you want someone to pay only a quarter for a rare book that was worth thousands of dollars? That said, not everyone needs an appraiser. The more complex your estate, the more likely you are to need someone to help you understand what your assets are worth, so that you can make decisions that are fair to everyone. In addition, please note that for an estate tax return, your heirs may need a licensed professional appraiser for some collectible items, paintings or jewelry.

- **The Captain of the Team:** This is you, of course—but you may opt to select one individual from the above list whose insights and advice you trust implicitly, and whose guidance you seek before making any major decision. That is your right as the captain.

- **Or none of the above.** You may choose not to partner with professionals to help you complete your estate plan but if you do opt to seek help, bear in mind that choosing the right professionals is critical.

You may be wondering why you would even consider assembling such a team, considering the potential expense involved. The answer is that the process of life and estate planning can be extremely confusing, frustrating, and costly to your heirs if you make a mistake. You want to not only avoid future mistakes, but also protect and maximize what you have already accumulated. Through their valuable advice, professionals oftentimes more than pay for themselves. You want to find the best qualified professionals you trust and can afford, given the size and complexity of your estate, and given what it is, specifically, that you are hoping to accomplish.

This guidebook will help you determine what you want to do and will give you a better sense of whether you need to work with qualified professionals and how to do so. Feel free to revisit this issue as necessary.

Our advice to you is simple: Talk to people you know and ask about their experience. Interview several professionals and ask yourself whether you like them, respect them, and trust them. Ask about the professional's experience; ask them to explain exactly what they can and cannot do for you. Beware of a professional who claims to be able to do everything. Last but not least, bear in mind that it is essential that you feel comfortable working with your team of trusted advisors.

We will look at the best criteria for choosing specific professionals a little later in this guidebook.

☐ **Complete the "Your People" worksheet on next page of this book.**

Your People

Executor

Name
Address
City/State/Zip
Telephone
Email

Financial Advisor

Name
Address
City/State/Zip
Telephone
Email

Attorney

Name
Address
City/State/Zip
Telephone
Email

Insurance Advisor

Name
Address
City/State/Zip
Telephone
Email

Clergy

Name
Address
City/State/Zip
Telephone
Email

Physician

Name
Address
City/State/Zip
Telephone
Email

Pharmacist

Name
Address
City/State/Zip
Telephone
Email

Durable Power of Attorney

Name
Address
City/State/Zip
Telephone
Email

Health Care Proxy

Name
Address
City/State/Zip
Telephone
Email

Accountant

Name
Address
City/State/Zip
Telephone
Email

Employer

Name
Address
City/State/Zip
Telephone
Email

Therapist

Name
Address
City/State/Zip
Telephone
Email

Dentist

Name
Address
City/State/Zip
Telephone
Email

Other

Name
Address
City/State/Zip
Telephone
Email

Section II:
Inventory: Your Assets
and Your Obligations

Where Is It?

"What do you own—and where is everything located?" These are important questions that your loved ones will need to be able to answer.

Amanda was in junior college and her sister, Lauren, was a senior in high school at the time of their father's passing. Their mom had died years earlier. Their father, Ryan, was the CEO of a successful construction business. When he died, they discovered that he left no instructions indicating his personal wishes, no will, and (crucially) no asset list. Amanda assumed responsibility for her younger sister and managing her father's affairs. Ryan was a private person who did not share much about his financial picture with anyone, and Amanda did not know where to start. She had absolutely no idea who his accountant was, who his attorney was, and who she should talk to at his company to learn about his business assets. She suddenly was responsible for closing a business and answering lots of questions that she knew nothing about. It took more than six years to locate and secure all her father's assets. It was and still remains a discovery process.

This situation would have been totally different if Ryan had taken the time to plan ahead and execute a will, and if he had shared with loved ones a detailed listing of his business interests and personal finances.

No one will ever know for sure why he did not plan better. It is hard to second-guess, but perhaps he felt his death was years or even decades away. Amanda and Lauren's experience is not unique and each day they are reminded of the value of planning. They have shared their story with the hope that others will learn from their experience.

Having a complete asset listing with detailed physical locations and specific instructions is a gift to your loved ones. Do not leave them to research (and perhaps give up on locating) the assets that have taken you a lifetime to accumulate.

- ☐ **Identify your assets—accurately and in writing—ahead of time.** Your assets should be clearly laid out in a single easy-to-access document. Beyond preparing and updating your will, this is the single most important preparatory step to take. If your loved ones do not know what assets you have or how to access them, you will increase exponentially the amount of work and effort necessary to settle your affairs. Keep the complete asset list in a safe place that more than one person has easy access to!

☐ **Complete the "Asset Inventory and Location" worksheet.** What assets comprise your estate? Use the "Asset Inventory and Location" worksheet you will find on the next page to get started on a rough draft that you can formalize later, and then update the list annually. Be sure to include any relevant items in each of the categories listed. Make multiple copies of this worksheet if necessary.

Asset Inventory and Location

For the Estate of _____

Executor's Name:

Date Checklist Completed:

Obtain copies of each of the following items and place in the same envelope as this Document Guide.

Legal Papers

- ❑ Will and/or trusts
- ❑ Letter of specific bequests
- ❑ Ethical will
- ❑ Deceased's final instructions, Disposition authorization, and/or Designated agent forms (sometimes included in an Advance Directive such as a Durable Power of Attorney for Health Care, or in a Living Will)
- ❑ Prepaid funeral contracts (cemetery plot information)
- ❑ Copy of driver's license
- ❑ Organ/tissue donation record
- ❑ Social Security card (or number)
- ❑ Birth certificates (of all family members)
- ❑ Marriage license or certificate
- ❑ Military service papers, including discharge records
- ❑ Domestic partnership registration
- ❑ Court documents for adoptions and divorce (including any property settlement agreements, name changes, prenuptial agreements, etc.)
- ❑ Community property agreements
- ❑ Passport, citizenship, immigration, and/or alien registration papers
- ❑ Pre-marital agreement

Personal Information

- ❑ Names and contact information of closest family and friends
- ❑ Names and contact information of all lawyers, accountants, doctors, etc.
- ❑ Family tree, if available (especially if there is no will)
- ❑ In-home safe (who has key/combination and access to it)

Financial Accounts: Primary and Contingent Beneficiary Designation Forms

- ❑ Bank accounts – checking, savings, CDs, etc.
- ❑ Investment/brokerage accounts, IRAs, 401(k), 403(b), SEP, HSA, FSA, etc.
- ❑ Stocks and bonds
- ❑ Annuities
- ❑ Nonqualified pension plan
- ❑ Credit and debit card accounts
- ❑ List of safety deposit boxes, where to find keys, and names of authorized users

Other Financial Records

- ❑ Survivor annuity benefit papers
- ❑ Employer/retirement benefit (pension) plans, pension/profit-sharing plans, etc.
- ❑ Veterans benefit records
- ❑ Disability payment documents (state, veterans, etc.)
- ❑ Income statements for the current year (Social Security, pension, IRAs, annuities, employment, and other income records)
- ❑ IRS income tax returns (for the current and previous year)
- ❑ IRS gift tax returns (if any, for all years)
- ❑ Property tax records and statements
- ❑ Business interests held, financial statements and agreements, contracts, etc.
- ❑ Loan papers
- ❑ Other (investment records, etc.)

Property, Deeds, Titles, and Promissory Notes/Loans

- ❑ Real estate property deeds (including any recent appraisals)
  - ❑ Primary home
  - ❑ Secondary home
  - ❑ Timeshare
  - ❑ Investment real estate
  - ❑ Commercial real estate
- ❑ Mortgage documents (including promissory/loan notes/discharge paperwork)
- ❑ Other promissory or loan notes (including loans owed to the deceased)
- ❑ Vehicle registrations (car, boat, RV, Jet Ski, etc.)
- ❑ Property leases
- ❑ Community care retirement agreement
- ❑ Storage unit (location and key)
- ❑ Collectibles (stamp collection, war medals, coin collections, etc.)
- ❑ Student loan (s) (protection rider)

Insurance Policies

- ❑ Life insurance
- ❑ Disability insurance
- ❑ Medical and dental insurance
- ❑ Health/dental insurance membership cards
- ❑ Long-term care insurance
- ❑ Homeowner's/rental insurance
- ❑ Auto insurance
- ❑ Umbrella liability insurance
- ❑ Other insurance
- ❑ Asset appraisals (jewelry)
- ❑ Accidental life insurance
- ❑ Veterans insurance
- ❑ Employers or pension insurance
- ❑ Funeral insurance (or other death-related benefit plans)
- ❑ Mortgage and/or credit insurance
- ❑ Credit card insurance (for balances)
- ❑ Workers' compensation insurance (and payment records)

☐ **Make sure the relevant documents are available and accessible in an emergency.** Be sure that family members and other important people know where to locate the most important documents. These documents should be filed in a secure, easily accessible place. In particular, note that *doctors must see important signed paperwork (healthcare power of attorney, healthcare proxy) at the time of administering care.* Otherwise, they may make decisions contrary to your wishes. Always provide a completed copy of your healthcare proxy document (also known as a durable power of attorney for health care) to both your proxy and your successor proxy.

Don't Make Them Struggle

Many families struggle to identify all the assets of an estate. This adds needless stress, worry, and conflict to an already difficult period in their lives. You can make this phase of the grieving process considerably easier by compiling a complete asset list, keeping it in a safe place, and making sure that more than one person in your inner circle knows where it is and has easy access to it. You do not want to cause people who are trying to carry out your wishes to feel unprepared to execute your plan.

Asset Ownership and Beneficiaries

It was a great day when Jessica and Ryan got married. They were childhood sweethearts who went off to college, met and married other people, and got divorced. They reconnected at their high school reunion, rekindled the flame, and got married a year later. During this joyous period, Jessica neglected to update her beneficiary designation. She fell into the common pattern of assuming that all of her assets were "taken care of."

Jessica died tragically in a skiing accident. Unfortunately, even though Jessica had remarried, she never changed the beneficiary designations on her retirement assets or her company-sponsored life insurance. Upon her death, her *ex-husband* received her life insurance death benefit directly and her current husband and ex-husband went into litigation over her employer-sponsored retirement plan.

Ryan knew that Jessica would never have wanted her ex-husband to receive the life insurance proceeds but that was completely out of his control because life insurance proceeds always go to the named beneficiary. As for Jessica's retirement plan, Ryan was able, with additional hassle and expense, to make the case that he never signed a waiver allowing Jessica's ex-husband to be named beneficiary of her retirement account at work. Federal law requires that a spouse must be the beneficiary of a qualified retirement plan such as a 401(k) unless the employee's spouse signs a waiver allowing someone else to be named. Since Ryan did not sign a waiver, he eventually received her retirement funds. But it took a lot of effort, time, and aggravation.

This story illustrates why it is essential to review your assets and beneficiary designations annually. Leaving an unintended beneficiary in place is an all-too-common mistake, one that can have a significant logistical, emotional, and personal impact on your affairs. Make sure your intended beneficiaries receive the funds you want them to receive.

- ☐ **Conduct regular beneficiary reviews.** It is more common than you might imagine for ex-spouses to enjoy payments from insurance policies and to even receive significant checks from retirement funds—all because an annual beneficiary review was not performed. This review allows you to notice when you have failed to change a beneficiary, a potentially devastating mistake that is not reversible after death. Another common overlooked mistake is when no beneficiary is named at all! When this information is left blank, the proceeds automatically go to the estate of the deceased.

- ☐ **Confirm the identities and whereabouts of all proposed beneficiaries of cash payments, life insurance, properties, IRAs, or other financial instruments.** Do this discreetly if the contents of your will have not yet been shared. Your executor needs to know who these people are and how to contact them. When the time comes, beneficiaries will need to be informed of their inheritance promptly so they can avoid potential tax problems. Update this list at least once a year.

Don't Forget to Name a Beneficiary

Amy was excited about her new job and on her first day completed her onboarding paperwork. She dutifully signed up for all benefits, including the 401(k) plan. The enrollment form asked for a beneficiary designation and their Social Security number. Amy wanted to name her sister as beneficiary but did not know her Social Security number so she temporarily left it blank until she could get the information. Because she never completed the form to officially name a beneficiary, her 401(k) plan had to be processed as an estate asset. After a lengthy delay, the money was disbursed to many people following Amy's passing, the complete opposite of her intended wishes.

It is important to note that a beneficiary's situation can change, and that you may need to reconsider your designation. For example, an intended beneficiary's ability to make sound financial decisions may have changed, or perhaps their living arrangements would be adversely affected if they unexpectedly received a financial windfall.

At the age of 25, Jason was able to move from his parents' home to a supervised living group home for mentally challenged adults. He loved his new environment and thrived in the community. Jason's father passed shortly after this move, and when his mother passed away four years later, their entire estate went to Jason outright. With this influx of assets he no longer qualified to receive state assistance. This meant that Jason was no longer able to participate in his woodworking job, a state-sponsored program that gave him joy and purpose.

Jason's parents meant well and never intended their assets to supplant him from state and federal benefits. Leaving their estate to Jason was meant to supplement his long-term needs. Proper planning would have avoided the chaos Jason experienced after their passing. These kinds of changes in circumstance need to be monitored and considered when you review your beneficiary designations. For many people, it makes sense to schedule the asset and beneficiary review annually, possibly to coincide with the annual tax filing.

Here are our recommendations for how to review your assets and beneficiaries:

- ☐ **Keep your asset totals private.** The amount of assets you possess will likely vary over time; therefore, it is a good idea not to share specific amounts with intended beneficiaries who may come to depend on the amount of anticipated inheritance.

- ☐ **Complete the "Beneficiary/Owner Inventory" worksheet.** Use this form, which appears on next page to conduct a regular review of your current choices regarding beneficiaries. Make sure that your choices are properly identified in your important documents. If the current choice is not the person who should be the beneficiary, make sure you change the named beneficiary on the document. It is important to list contingent beneficiaries as well.

Beneficiary/Owner Inventory

Legal Documents

- ❑ Will
- ❑ Trust

Insurance Policies

- ❑ Life insurance
- ❑ Disability
- ❑ Accidental life insurance
- ❑ Veterans insurance
- ❑ Employers group insurance
- ❑ Retiree group insurance
- ❑ Funeral insurance (or other death-related benefit plans)
- ❑ Mortgage and/or credit insurance
- ❑ Credit card insurance (for balances)
- ❑ Long-term care insurance
- ❑ Workers' compensation insurance (and payment records)

Financial Accounts

- ❑ Bank accounts—checking, savings, CDs, etc.
- ❑ HSA/FSA/dependent care
- ❑ Investment/brokerage accounts, IRAs, 401(k)s, etc.
- ❑ Stocks and bonds
- ❑ Annuities
- ❑ Deferred compensation
- ❑ Cash balance plans
- ❑ Stock option plans
- ❑ Safety deposit box (who is authorized to access)

☐ **Confirm both ownership and successor ownership of all assets.**
It is crucial that you make sure proper ownership is in place for
your assets. For example, if you own a 529 account (a tax-advan-
taged savings plan designed to encourage saving for future college costs) for your child, make sure to list a successor owner so
that upon your death, the successor owner will assume responsibility for the account and will be able to direct the assets toward
the intended beneficiary of the 529 plan.

The following story illustrates just how important it is to double-check
beneficiary listings.

Janice loved her job. She spent 20 years working for a local YWCA, a non-
profit with a mission focused on eliminating racism and empowering
women. Although she did not receive a huge salary, she did receive great
benefits. She dutifully participated in open enrollment every year and contributed to her 403(b) retirement plan. She was a divorced, single mother
of two. She thought that her children were the beneficiaries of her retirement account, but when she got divorced, she forgot to officially change the
designation. At the time of her death, Janice's ex-husband was still listed
as beneficiary. Even though her will specified that her two children were
to inherit her assets and divide them equally, her retirement account went
directly to her ex-husband because she had not updated the beneficiary
form. Regardless of what you say in your will or trust, assets will pass to
whomever is designated as the beneficiary. You must be very careful to
ensure that the beneficiary designations on your assets are up to date and
accurately reflect your wishes!

As you have seen, there are many situations when an individual may unin-
tentionally leave contradictory instructions about how assets should be
distributed. The result is stress, chaos, and confusion for the family.

Digital Assets

Today's cell phones, computers, and social media accounts store vital information that people may need to access after the death of a loved one. It is important to provide a means of getting to this information and to make your wishes known concerning shutting down all relevant accounts.

Discuss the following subjects during planning sessions with your inner circle:

- ☐ **Make sure your cell phone is locked or password-protected.** Provide at least one trusted person with information on how to access the phone in case of an emergency.

- ☐ **Confirm whether there are messages, photos, and/or videos on the phone that you want to save or protect.** If so, these should be backed up regularly onto an external hard drive.

- ☐ **Confirm what you want to have happen to your cell phone and the media on it once you are gone.** You may, for instance, want a spouse or family member to have access to messages and photos on the phone. Record your wishes in writing. If you want use of the phone to pass to someone else (such as a spouse), discuss the billing and transfer arrangements and also put that in writing.

- ☐ **Confirm whether your computer and/or tablet computer are password-protected.** If so, tell at least one trusted person how to access the computer in case of an emergency.

- ☐ **Online social media sites:** Do you want your pictures and videos to remain online? Should your family or loved ones have access to them? Where are they held? What is the password? If you want to share this information, make a point of doing so and share the appropriate passwords.

- ☐ **Complete the "Digital Asset Inventory" worksheet.** You can find it on next page of this book.

Digital Asset Inventory

Device	Website	Username	Password
Computer – Home			
Computer – Office			
Cell Phone			
iPad			
iCloud			

Email Accounts	Email Address	Username	Password

Social Networks	Website	Username	Password	Disposition Desires
Facebook				
LinkedIn				
Twitter				
Google				
Instagram				
Snapchat (photo vault)				
Dating Profile/Website				
Digital Subscriptions				
○ Amazon				
○ Airlines				
○ Uber				
○ Lyft				
○ Newspapers				
Other				

Planning Ahead: Your Facebook Account

Susan was grief-stricken by the loss of her youngest daughter, Elizabeth, who died in a car accident. Susan often looked at her daughter's Facebook account to see her pictures. What she did not realize was that her daughter's Facebook account had been hacked and someone had added pictures and was sending messages such as, "How are you, how's the family? Been a while. Don't miss me too much." Susan was devastated. If you do not want your loved ones to have to go through something traumatic like that, you need to leave instructions for your social media accounts.

Over a billion people use Facebook, the world's leading social media platform. If you are one of them, here is a question you should consider closely: What will happen to your Facebook account after you pass away? The answer is: It is up to you. Here are the options:

- ☐ **Decide whether you want your account memorialized or deleted after your passing.** Facebook allows you to either appoint a legacy contact to look after your memorialized account or to have your account permanently deleted. If you do not choose to have your account permanently deleted, it will be memorialized once Facebook becomes aware of your passing. Facebook strongly suggests setting up a legacy contact so your account can be managed once it is memorialized.

Is a Memorialized Account Right for You?

Memorialized accounts allow friends and family to gather and share memories after someone who was a Facebook user has passed away. If you opt to set up a memorialized account, the word "Remembering" will be shown next to your name on the profile after your passing. Depending on the privacy settings you choose for the account, your friends can share memories on the memorialized time-line, and content you shared (such as posts and photos) will stay on Facebook and be visible to the audience you chose to share it with. Note that memorialized profiles do not appear in Facebook's public spaces, such as in suggestions for People You May Know.

- ☐ **If you opt for a memorialized account, choose a legacy contact.** You can add, change, or remove your legacy contact in your Facebook account's General Settings at any time. To add a legacy contact, just log in to your Facebook account, select Settings, then click Manage Account. Type in the name of the Facebook friend you want to be your legacy contact and click Add. To let your friend know he or she is now your legacy contact, click Send. If you want to change or remove a legacy contact, all you have to do is log in, click Manage Account, type in your friend's name, then click Remove. From there, you can add a new legacy contact if you want to. When your account is memorialized, your legacy contact will be notified.

- ☐ **Understand what a legacy contact can do.** A legacy contact looks after your account if it is memorialized. Once your account is memorialized, your legacy contact will have the option to do things like update your profile picture and cover photo, or write a pinned post for your profile (for example, to share a final message on your behalf or to provide information about a memorial service). Your legacy contact will also be able to respond to new friend requests (for example, old friends or family members who were not yet on Facebook when your account was memorialized). Your legacy contact can also request the removal of your account. Please note, however, that if your timeline and tagging settings do not allow anyone other than you to post on your timeline, your legacy contact will not be able to add a pinned post to your profile once it is memorialized.

☐ **Understand what your legacy contact cannot do.** Your legacy contact cannot log in to your account; remove or change past posts, photos, and other things shared on your timeline; read your messages; remove any of your friends; make new friend requests; or add a new legacy contact to your account.

☐ **Decide whether your Facebook account should be deleted upon your passing.** Facebook allows you to have your account permanently deleted after you die. For directions on how to make this preselection, please follow instructions through Facebook. com.

Planning Ahead: Your Google Account

Google offers an extremely easy-to-use tool, the Inactive Account Manager, which allows you choose what will happen if you are unexpectedly unable to use your Google Account, such as in the event of an accident or death.

Use the Inactive Account Manager. You can use this tool to decide exactly how long Google must wait before terminating your account due to inactivity and identify up to 10 people for Google to notify when your Google Account becomes inactive. You can also give these people access to some of your data. To set up your Inactive Account Manager plan, visit this website: https://myaccount.google.com/u/0/inactive

Planning Ahead: Your Twitter Account

Twitter does not currently offer any planning tools that allow users to decide ahead of time what will happen to their accounts in the event of death.

☐ **Tell someone you trust your plan for Twitter.** As of this writing, the best way to plan for Twitter is to share your login information with a trusted individual and give that person instructions to delete your account on your behalf after you have passed away. Alternatively, your family can present Twitter with a death certificate and request that your account be deactivated.

Planning Ahead: Your Instagram Account

Instagram's approach to supporting users who want to plan ahead is similar to Facebook's approach.

☐ **Understand your planning options on Instagram.** You may opt to give a trusted immediate family member your Instagram login information so they can simply delete the account on your behalf after your passing. Alternatively, you can let a specific family member know that you want them to be the one who either reports the account for memorialization or requests that the account be removed from Instagram.

Memorializing an Instagram account simply means it cannot be changed. This includes changes to likes, followers, tags, posts, and comments. Instagram does not allow anyone to log into a memorialized account. The profile of a memorialized account does not appear differently from an account that has not been memorialized. Posts that the deceased person shared, including photos and videos, stay on Instagram and are visible to the audience they were shared with. Memorialized accounts do not appear in public spaces, such as the Explore section.

Instagram makes an effort to prevent references to memorialized accounts from appearing on Instagram in ways that may be upsetting to the person's friends and family, and it also takes measures to protect the privacy of the deceased person by securing the account. Instagram requires proof of death, such as a link to an obituary or news article, to memorialize an account.

Verified immediate family members can also request the removal of a loved one's account from Instagram. When a request for removal is submitted,

Instagram requires proof that the person making the request is an immediate family member of the deceased. Typically, this proof includes the following:

- The deceased person's birth certificate

- The deceased person's death certificate

- Proof of authority under local law that the person requesting removal is the lawful representative of the deceased person or his/her estate

Note: Instagram *will not* provide login information for a memorialized account.

Section III: Estate Planning

Choose Your Legacy

Just about everyone is familiar with at least one or two songs by the pop star Prince. His hits "Purple Rain," "Little Red Corvette," "1999," and "Delirious" are played on radio stations and playlists around the world. What you may not be quite as familiar with is the fact that Prince died without leaving a will. The official term for this is "dying intestate."

Prince passed away at the age of 57, alone and unresponsive in his Paisley Park estate. He left no instructions for the disposition of his property in the event of his passing. This left his family and friends with a sprawling, complex, extremely expensive set of legal and logistical problems to manage. It will take years to untangle his estate. In the meantime, his relatives and the people in his inner circle are dealing with a chaotic mess. They are not only faced with the difficult challenge of determining how Prince would have wanted his affairs settled, but also saddled with the high-stakes decision of whether to hire attorneys and professional advisors to defend their interests. His estate is valued at over $300 million; the disputes are likely to be ugly and costly for everyone involved.

We share this story not to reinforce something you probably already know—that squabbles over who gets what in big estates can be the cause of much conflict, confusion, and grief—but rather to impress upon you the reality that even in much smaller estates, a lack of information about the intentions of the deceased can cause things to get ugly quickly. Dying intestate makes things far more difficult than they have to be for friends and family.

Prince was an eccentric person. We do not know whether he meant to leave those who were close to him in a state of confusion, insecurity, and ongoing conflict. We do know that *you* don't have to leave *your* friends and loved ones in that state. If chaos and hefty attorney's bills are not the legacy you mean to leave for those who matter most to you, then you will want to consider the next items on the checklist closely.

Plan ahead and avoid the classic problems that are most likely to create a burden for those you leave behind. Such burdens typically include financial and tax problems, difficulties with the transfer of assets, unresolved questions about the care of minor children, and long-term conflicts among heirs. If you are not careful, these issues can end up being your legacy—even if your estate is not quite the size of Prince's!

Legal Documents

Your primary objective in completing and updating legal documents is to ensure that your assets go to the people you want to receive them, and that your wishes about what you care about most are known if you pass away or are unable, for whatever reason, to make important decisions for yourself.

There is a typical "suite of documents" recommended for estate planning that includes a will, advance directive, healthcare proxy, power of attorney, and revocable trust. Very few people have all of these documents up-to-date. That is why we see so many instances of "if only they had known." In this section of the book, we will address each document, its purpose, and its importance in your planning process. As you read what follows, please consider the consequences of not having these documents in place, and the tremendous gift you are giving to your family when your personal affairs are in order and your wishes are clearly articulated.

If You Become Unable to Make Your Own Decisions

Here is the critical question. *If you become unable to make your own decisions … what will your family and loved ones do?*

Advance healthcare planning is a way to plan for and share your wishes for future medical treatment in the event you are incapacitated and cannot communicate. The advance healthcare directive (also referred to as an advance directive or medical directive) allows you to identify two important things: your desired treatment road map and the person designated to act on your behalf. This document identifies formal instructions for physicians about what treatment you do and do not want. Even if you have discussed your preferred care with your family it is critical to specify your wishes in writing in a legally binding document. If you don't, you are at risk of your treatment wishes not being recognized. In some states this road map is called a living will. You can name the person who can make medical decisions on your behalf though a durable power of attorney for health care (often known as your healthcare proxy). Consult an attorney to determine which approach makes sense based on your situation and where you live, travel, and may receive treatment.

The Advance Directive - Your Treatment Road Map

In many states this document is known as a living will. It identifies the medical treatment you want and the treatment you would not want to receive when in certain states of health. Addressing such issues may seem overwhelming, but is it critical, even if you have no current health concerns. This document is a gift of direction for your loved ones, who may otherwise be torn about what to do.

Decide, ahead of time and in writing, how the most important medical decisions should be made if you cannot make them. These decisions include directions about pain medication; directions about when to provide, deny, or withdraw artificial nutrition and hydration, as well as all other forms of medical care, including cardiopulmonary resuscitation (CPR); and directions about organ donation in the event of death. Ideally, these decisions should be shared with appropriate family members well in advance of any medical emergency.

Make Your Wishes Known and Your Documents Accessible

We have been privy to some complicated and disappointing situations relating to advance healthcare directives, including one in which doctors continued resuscitation measures when that was clearly against the person's wishes. Why? The family was unable to bring the advance healthcare directive that the doctors needed to see. The loved ones knew their loved one's wishes but did not know where the documentation was. No one had told them.

The lesson learned was this: It is important to not only make your wishes about medical care known in writing, but also to make sure that family members have easy access to a physical copy they can show physicians at the right moment. It can be very difficult to get members of the medical establishment to reverse a course of treatment once it has begun.

In addition to making sure people have access to the documents they will need, we strongly recommend that you *discuss* with your inner circle the question of who can and cannot make medical decisions on your behalf when you are unable to do so for yourself. This is not always easy, and yet it is critically important that others understand your desires if you are unable to make decisions or you have specific requests for end-of-life planning. It may be worthwhile to include physicians and/or clergy in these discussions.

In particular, you will want to discuss the specifics of your advance healthcare directive with your family. It's impossible to predict every possible scenario, but consider the following plausible situations:

- You are involved in an accident and are unconscious.

- You are in a coma without any hope of recovery.

- You have suffered brain damage or severe dis-ease but are not suffering from a terminal illness.

- You have suffered brain damage or severe disease and are also suffering from a terminal illness.

Such questions are not pleasant to consider, but they will be even more difficult for your loved ones to navigate alone than they are for you to discuss together. It makes sense to use an advance healthcare directive to minimize the logistical, emotional, and psychological impacts upon family members. Without this document, your loved ones may well be called upon to address these complex issues at a time of high personal stress without any sense of what your wishes and preferences are.

A popular downloadable living will known as the "Five Wishes" document proposes the following topics, which are an excellent starting point:

- The Person I Want to Make Care Decisions for Me When I Can't

- The Kind of Medical Treatment I Want or Don't Want

- How Comfortable I Want to Be

- How I Want People to Treat Me

- What I Want My Loved Ones to Know

For more information about the "Five Wishes" living will, visit www.fivewishes.org.

☐ **Consider addressing specific religious beliefs directly in your documents.** If your family follows a particular religious teaching relative to medical care in emergency situations, you should consider addressing your explicit wishes with regard to following or disregarding these teachings in the advance healthcare directive. For example, some religious institutions regard the withdrawal of health care in the event of severe brain damage as morally wrong; if you disagree, an advance healthcare directive that confirms your disagreement in writing will provide an opportunity to state this explicitly for the benefit of your family members.

☐ **Consider contacting these organizations for additional guidance on advance healthcare directives.** They may be able to provide more in-depth advice that is directly relevant to your situation.

- Eldercare Locator, a public service of the US Administration on Aging connecting to services for older adults and their families: https://eldercare.acl.gov/Public/Index.aspx

- National Hospice and Palliative Care Organization: www.nhpco.org

- National Institute on Aging (advance care planning resources): https://www.nia.nih.gov/health/caregiving/advance-care-planning

- US Government Information on Organ Donation and Transplantation: https://organdonor.gov/index.html

☐ **Review your advance healthcare directive regularly.** We recommend that you review your advance healthcare directive annually. You can revoke or revise your advance healthcare directive and durable power of attorney for health care at any time.

The Person You Choose

The individual you identify as your healthcare power of attorney can also be known as your healthcare proxy, attorney-in-fact, medical power of attorney, healthcare surrogate, or by any number of other names, depending on the state. Most commonly referred to as your healthcare proxy, this person can make healthcare decisions on your behalf if you are no longer able to. When your advance directive goes into effect varies by state. Naming this person ensures that he or she, and not the doctors or someone you did not want to make decisions, can have the final say in your healthcare.

☐ **Specify the level of authority the person named as your durable power of attorney (POA) for health care (your healthcare proxy) will have.** Among the important questions to address are the following: When will the authority take effect? Will your healthcare POA have access to medical records? Will your POA be able to transfer you to another medical facility? Will your POA be able to transfer you to another state? Will your POA be able to personally sign off on a "Do Not Resuscitate" order, even if family members object? Will your POA be able to authorize an autopsy, dispose of remains, and donate all or part of your body to transplant, research, or education facilities, even if family members object?

☐ **Indicate whether you want a Do Not Resuscitate (DNR) order.** A DNR is not a legal document but rather an order to not perform CPR if your heart stops. You, or your healthcare proxy, have to meet with your doctor to complete the form together because your doctor must sign this order telling other professionals to not perform CPR. If you have done this, make sure your loved ones know and the document is visible and accessible. A DNR *cannot* name an individual to make decisions on your behalf.

☐ **If you are seriously ill, you or your healthcare proxy may also want to consider a physician order for life-sustaining treatment (POLST).** This is not a legal document and does not replace an advance directive. Rather, it is a medical order that can complement an advance directive with additional specific medical orders during a medical emergency. A POLST can be appropriate for those diagnosed with advanced illness or frailty. A POLST cannot name a person to make medical decisions on your behalf.

☐ **If you are a registered organ donor, prior to completing your advance directive, you will want to confirm that your wishes for organ and tissue donation and the limits you placed on their use are consistent with what's in the advance directive.** If you are unsure whether you have registered as an organ donor, your status may be indicated by a red heart on your driver's license. You can visit organdonor.gov or registerme.org to access your registration record. Because state-registered organ donation is a legally binding decision, it is important to talk to your family members about your decision.

Healthcare Power of Attorney

Bob was 19 years old and a standout varsity lacrosse player. During a playoff game he went head-to-head with the opposing team and was knocked out cold with a concussion. He was rushed to the local hospital in stable condition and his parents were called. Because he was over 18, Bob's parents were unable to get information about his medical records and had no authority to make decisions for him because he did not have a healthcare POA.

☐ **Make sure a Health Insurance Portability and Accountability Act (HIPAA) authorization is signed.** The HIPAA authorization form is **required when private healthcare information** is provided to third-party individuals or entities **not involved directly with the patient's care or billing for that care.** Without this authorization, someone acting as agent will not have access to medical records and information and doctors will be unable to discuss the details of your medical condition with them.

☐ **Ask an attorney what will happen if no healthcare proxy is identified.** This will vary by state.

Advance Health Care Regulations Vary by State

Ensuring that your advance healthcare plan is legal without the help of an attorney can be confusing because advance healthcare regulations vary by state. Depending where you live, travel, or receive treatment you may need multiple forms to formalize your intentions. If you live in multiple states, you may need multiple documents, all of which should be checked for consistency. To see how these documents vary by state, visit https://www.aarp.org/caregiving/financial-legal/free-printable-advance-directives/.

Power of Attorney and Financial Decisions

As a decision making instrument related to finances, a durable power of attorney (POA) document allows you to name someone to make legal and financial decisions on your behalf if you are no longer able to do so. Note that this POA can act on your behalf only while you are living.

The reason this document is so important is that if you become incapacitated without having named a POA, no one can legally help manage your financial affairs. A durable POA would be active upon signing the legal documents and would grant the designated individual the power to assist you with everything from paying bills to filing tax returns and making sure bank accounts are properly managed.

Consider the case of a son who helps his parents manage their retirement income so they can be comfortable staying in their home. He pays their utilities and all other expenses. If he became incapacitated without a named POA, who would step in to continue that support to his parents?

Or what if one of the parents falls ill and has not completed a POA?

In each case, the other family members are left helpless to assist and manage important financial affairs.

☐ **Ask for an attorney's guidance on whether the executor of the will should be the same person who has POA.** The executor is the person named in a will who controls distribution of net assets after death (money and property distribution and creditor repayment), according to a person's final wishes. A power of attorney document identifies someone, often called the agent or attorney-in-fact, to handle issues for a person while he or she is still alive. As a practical matter, a POA ceases to be effective at death. There are advantages and disadvantages to naming the same person as the executor and the power of attorney. One potential downside is that someone with an interest in the distribution of assets pre- but not post-death may not always make decisions that appear fair to others, and there is the potential for self-serving choices that do not preserve money for other heirs. An advantage to such an approach, however, could be that a family member who was extremely close to you may be able to make better decisions in unforeseen circumstances, decisions that you would have endorsed. Ask your attorney to review the duties and responsibilities involved so that you can make a choice you feel comfortable with. Once the decision is made, be sure to put it in writing and communicate clearly about who is responsible for what.

The Value of Wills

To understand just how important wills are, we need to look closely at a specific legal concept: probate.

Probate and Wills

You have probably heard the word "probate" before, but you may be unclear about precisely what that word means. The granting of probate is typically the first step in the legal process of administering the estate of a person who has passed away. Probate is meant to resolve all outstanding claims against the estate and ensure the proper distribution of the decedent's property by means of a will. When someone dies intestate (without leaving a will), or without making it known whether he or she left a will, the result is usually confusion, chaos, and stress for the family and loved ones.

☐ **Purpose of a Will.** A will serves as a legally binding document that gives you control of what happens and, just as important, what *does not* happen to your estate upon your passing. A will makes the management and final distribution of your assets and wishes very clear. Absence of a will means there is no guarantee your wishes will be followed. If you have not written a will yet, then this is the best place to start to identify your wishes. A qualified attorney can help you get this done; alternatively, you may opt to do the will yourself with help from any number of easily accessed online programs and materials. Your will is where you decide how your assets should be distributed and who the guardian for your children will be. There is certainly value in paying a professional to help with this, but if you choose not to, there is plenty of other guidance available that may help you complete the task yourself.

☐ **If you create the will yourself, have it notarized.** This is important because every state has a different requirement for self-made wills. You want your will to be "self-proving" to move through legal channels faster. A will that is not properly witnessed and notarized is likely to be declared invalid.

☐ **Keep your will up to date.** Wills must be reviewed periodically to account for life changes such as the birth of a child, the death of a beneficiary, marriage, divorce, or the serious illness of a spouse or child. Any lifestyle event that causes your wishes to change should be the catalyst for revising your will. If you decide to make a revision to your will, be sure to date it and notify at least one person where to find the most up-to-date copy. It is important to dispose of old wills so that there is no confusion regarding which will is the most recent and valid.

Your Last Will and Testament

Your will identifies your beneficiaries, executor, guardians (when applicable), and specific instructions on distribution of your assets. Without a will the state will settle your estate in accordance with its predetermined guidelines, which usually takes additional time and expense. With a will, the executor will safeguard your assets and handle the distribution in accordance with the written wishes.

☐ **Select your executor and let them know they are the named person to execute the settling of your estate.** This is extremely important.

Is Your Executor Up to the Task?

Make sure the person you select as executor of your will is up to the task and understands the importance of getting appropriate advice and assistance when needed. We have seen plenty of instances when people who were not prepared to take on the responsibility of acting as the executor failed to get good advice—and then made a series of poor decisions, like liquidating property and selling short. The lesson here is an important one: An executor should be willing to get help from time to time and should not assume he or she has the responsibility to do everything without any assistance or guidance from outsiders.

☐ **Legal Guardianship: If there are minor children in your life, make sure you have identified in your will your choice of legal guardian for them.** This must be done thoughtfully and with due consideration for the legal requirements of your state. Review your guardian selections regularly; we recommend once a year. Someone who was qualified to act as guardian when you set up your will may not be as qualified a year or two later if their personal circumstance change. Bear in mind that someone who has been named as a child's godparent *is not* automatically that child's legal guardian.

The Godparent Question

True or False: The people you select as godparents will become your children's legal guardians if something happens to you. Many people assume the right answer here is "True," which is incorrect.

Matt and Katie were a young couple with two lovely girls, Jessica (11) and Julianna (8). Both girls were baptized at the church that Katie had grown up in. At the time of each baptism, they had asked their friends Mark and Lisa to act as the godparents, and Mark and Lisa had agreed. They were amazing godparents—happily married, heavily involved in the girls' lives, and active in the church. They had known Katie and Matt for more than a decade and were close friends. Matt and Katie felt they were the perfect choice to watch over their children if anything were to happen to the two of them before Jessica and Julianna became independent adults.

Then came the day when Matt and Katie took the girls on a day trip up to the mountains to go swimming. Matt took a tight turn too wide and caused a head-on collision with an RV. Matt was killed on impact, and Katie died a few hours later at the hospital.

Both girls survived with serious injuries. The physical injuries would heal in time, but what wouldn't heal were the emotional wounds of losing both parents at such a young age. Traumatized, the girls relied on their godparents, who spent shifts staying in the hospital with them every day until they were discharged.

Mark and Lisa assumed that the next step would be to find some way to confirm their legal guardianship of the girls. But Matt and Katie had never appointed a legal guardian for their children and there was no documentation of their wishes. So the judge made the decision and appointed Matt's brother, Eric, as legal guardian, which did not coincide with what Matt and Katie would have wanted.

You could argue that Eric was not the best choice: he lived in a small apartment, usually worked 12 hours a day, and seemed to have little time to spend with the girls and to take care of day-to-day tasks. Mark and Lisa were troubled by rumors they heard that Eric spent long nights out drinking with his friends. They felt certain that he was not the person Matt and Katie would have chosen to take care of their daughters. But the judge had the final say and he chose the person who was "next in line" in the family. Eric agreed to be the guardian, and there was nothing to be done.

Selecting someone as a godparent is not a legally binding act. Your wishes will not be taken into consideration if you do not take the next step to formally document your choice of guardian(s) and make that choice binding by including it in your will. Do not leave a detail like this to chance. Be sure to formally identify your preferred guardians for your children.

☐ **Make certain that the person(s) you have selected as legal guardian and successor guardian know they were named.** This responsibility should not come as a surprise after your death.

☐ **Make sure the guardians know where to find the documents they need.** This includes your will and anything else you want them to have. Much like your own inner circle and inventory list, guardians should be left with information on the children's doctors, schools, and all other pertinent information. You can also leave a Letter to Guardians sharing your values and your hopes for your children.

☐ **Remember that you have the option to select one person to raise the children and another to manage the money.** The Guardian of the Person is the individual you would like to raise your child(ren) if you should die. The Guardian of the Estate would handle the finances for your child(ren). This distinction helps if you are hesitating because the person who has the best bond with your children, and whom you would name guardian in a heartbeat, is not so great with money. You can choose a separate Guardian of the Estate, someone you know to be fiscally responsible, to manage the children's financial well-being with only the children's best interests in mind.

☐ **You also have the option to give a description of who you would absolutely *not* want to be named guardian of your children and why.** It is unlikely the court would get to this point if you have named a guardian and successor guardian. However, if the person(s) you have appointed decide to decline the responsibility of raising your children, it can be helpful for a judge to know your perspective on anyone you feel is not a good choice. The judge is required to act in the child's best interest.

The Value of Trusts

Clients commonly ask whether they need a trust. Often, the answer is yes, and the reason a living trust is typically included in the typical suite of estate planning documents. It is a common misconception that only the wealthy need a trust. Trusts are often used to distribute assets that would otherwise be subject to the oversight of probate court. Placing your assets in a trust can help you avoid probate.

> ### Trust Basics - Revocable versus Irrevocable
>
> A living trust, sometimes called "inter vivos" or "grantor revocable" trust, is different from a will for two main reasons. First, it provides privacy, and second, it allows you to avoid probate by naming assets to go into the trust either through ownership change, re-deeding, or naming the trust as the beneficiary.

This is something you maintain control over during your lifetime. A living trust becomes irrevocable (unchangeable) upon your death. You can also create an irrevocable trust during your lifetime, which is advisable in some estates for tax planning purposes. An irrevocable trust is also private and allows you to avoid probate; the difference between an irrevocable and revocable (living) trust is that in the former trust, you give up control during your lifetime. Both of these documents should be drafted with the help of a qualified attorney.

Trusts can also be used to detail specific wishes or when the goal is to protect beneficiaries. For instance, a special-needs child may lose benefits and income from other sources as a result of inheriting money directly. In such a case, a trust should be set up to protect the beneficiary.

You may want to talk to an attorney and/or a qualified financial advisor about whether a trust is appropriate for your situation. Do not get lost in the legalese; have a discussion about your ultimate intentions and the varying circumstances likely to be faced. A trust may be a streamlined way to help you accomplish some of your goals.

A Trust Would Have Been a Better Choice

Diane and Rob, always referred to as the "fun aunt and uncle", took great pride in being active in the lives of their nieces and nephews. They decided that, should anything happen to one of them, they wanted everything to pass to the other. Then they had to determine what would happen if they passed at the same time. They decided that in this situation they wanted everything to go their nieces and nephews for education and for certain trips and experiences they would have liked to have made possible for their nieces and nephews if they had still been alive. Diane and Rob originally set up their paperwork so that the nieces and nephews on both sides of the family were equal contingent beneficiaries on their insurance policies, investments, and retirement plans, but they were unsure who would get the death benefits and accounts, and at what age, if they named their young nieces and nephews directly. They didn't want the money to be held by an insurance company until the minors reached a certain age. They thought about naming their own siblings as distributors of these funds, but weren't confident about how they handled their finances.

Some of their siblings were big spenders, not savers, and Diane and Rob wanted to make sure the money would be available for the children's education. They met with an attorney to discuss their ultimate goals and objectives, drafted a trust, and named a trustee to carry out their wishes. They were able to include the house and assets in the trust, which helped them confirm that their assets would go where they wanted them to go in the event that they both died at the same time. However, as they were setting up this trust, Diane and Rob also became aware of several potential outcomes they hadn't even considered. If one of them died first, there was no guarantee that the other would then distribute the combined estate to the nieces and nephews on both sides of the family equally and without squabble. The attorney also asked them to address what they would want if some of their nieces and nephews had already finished college before the distribution. What should the money be used for? Should it be given to them outright? Diane and Rob were able to put down exactly what they wanted in the trust, and they now feel extremely confident that if anything happens to them, they will have a major positive impact on the lives of their nieces and nephews through their planned legacy.

Should You Set Up a Trust?

Ask yourself whether family members can handle the responsibility of managing the assets being passed to them. Would a trust that allows others to serve as gatekeepers and protectors of the assets be appropriate?

Trusts are often necessary when assets pass to a spouse in a second marriage, when minor beneficiaries are involved, and in any situation where it is important to control the means by which assets are distributed and passed to beneficiaries. Common reasons to use a trust vehicle are to mitigate taxes, to control the timing flow of assets, for more confidentiality, for enhanced organization, and for the precise disposition of certain assets.

You may want to consider the use of co-trustees, with the idea that each trustee brings some important qualities and skills to their position (e.g., one family member to deal with the child(ren)'s development and another trustee to focus on the proper investment of the trust's funds). In this case, you might name two or three successors to each appointed trustee and provide a mechanism to fill any vacancies that might occur in the future.

You can also plan for the possible removal of a trustee if necessary, or consider giving someone a limited power of appointment to change the ultimate disposition of the trust. One scenario where this may be appropriate is for a couple with small children who want to relinquish control over the trust at a certain age. The trust might provide that the assets pass to the children at the age of 25 upon the death of the surviving spouse. But what if the child is experiencing a serious medical issue, or for some other reason is unable to manage the money properly? What if the child has simply become a spendthrift? If the surviving spouse has a limited power of appointment over the trust, he or she could change the disposition to account for such unexpected issues.

- ☐ **Ask an attorney's advice on whether bequests should be made to specific beneficiaries or to a trust.** Disclose all relevant information for each beneficiary and get the accountant's and attorney's feedback about each one. There are tax implications that can arise when bequests are not made correctly.

- ☐ **Select your trustee and let them know they have been selected.** Make sure your trustee understands the duties and responsibilities in accordance with your selected trust provisions.

- ☐ **Fund the trusts that have been set up.** It is a tragic but common mistake: people talk with attorneys about setting up a trust for a loved one and then assume that the attorney will take care of the administrative work necessary to ensure that the intended funds or property go into the trust without realizing that the attorney expects the client to take this action. We have encountered several situations where people died with unfunded trusts. That sad outcome leaves the family to deal with unfinished business, creating anxiety and disappointment for the beneficiaries. Work with your financial advisor to make sure the titling of your assets is accurate and current and matches the wording used in your trust documents.

- ☐ **Trust disbursements.** If there is an irrevocable trust in place that involves gifting to named beneficiaries of the trust, ask about the plan for disbursements after death. If the trust owns and is beneficiary of a life insurance policy, for example, the trust will receive the insurance proceeds after the death of the loved one. Ask whether there are provisions for spousal access. If the goal was to remove money from the estate inventory (to avoid inflating the size of the estate at death), ask for a review of the gifting strategy. Verify that the appropriate annual notifications to each beneficiary have been done and that your tax returns reflect the provisions of the trust. The notice to the beneficiaries is known as a "Crummey letter" and it must be sent out annually. There are many ways to void a "qualified irrevocable trust" for estate tax reasons, and mistakes in this area can lead to major tax obligations. Make sure your professional advisory team, attorney, CPA, and financial advisor all know their roles so things like the Crummey letters do not get missed.

☐ **Keep the lines of communication open.** Beware! There are many ways to mishandle a trust that can leave your estate—and by extension your family—grappling with major unanticipated tax obligations. Many of these mistakes arise from not keeping your inner circle people up to date on your gifting strategy and decisions. The most typical problem in estate planning is lack of communication between professionals. Sometimes a person executes appropriate changes with their lawyer or accountant without informing the other, needlessly complicating execution. Be sure all your advisors are in the loop and are communicating with one another, and with you, about what you want, why you want it, and how best to achieve it.

☐ **Periodically review all legal documents with an attorney.** Once you update your attorney on your goals and the steps you have already taken, you will probably also want to seek advice about any changes to your bequest plans that may be necessary. Such a review may include:

- *The will status and beneficiary designations.* Confirm when the most recent will was signed and recorded; share the Beneficiary Audit Checklist you completed, confirm that the attorney has a copy of this, and confirm that the beneficiary designations are accurate and up to date. If there are beneficiaries who are legally regarded as minors in the state in which they live, this will need to be addressed. Note that the legal age of majority varies by state.

- *Trusts.* Get the attorney's informed professional advice on the important question of whether to establish a trust.

- *Estate planning issues.* Depending on the complexity of your estate, you may decide that it makes sense to include your attorney in this discussion. Estate planning is the process of anticipating and arranging for the management and disposal of your property after your death while minimizing tax obligations. If it makes economic sense for the attorney to help you with this, you will want to share the "big picture" vision of what you would like to see happen to your property with him or her.

Important Issues to Raise About Legal Documents

Here are some special considerations you will want to take into account as you square away your legal documents.

☐ **Pay special attention to citizenship of beneficiaries and those who have been appointed roles in your estate planning documents.** Non-US citizens may face major logistical and financial hurdles in claiming direct bequests. It is a good idea to talk to an attorney and/or a tax professional about whether it makes more sense to establish a trust for such individuals.

Confirm Citizenship!

Alysa and Randy had been married for 56 years when Randy passed away from natural causes. They had both emigrated from Poland, and they loved to share stories with their family about their lives there. Randy was 79 years old when he died, and Alysa was 78. The couple assured their children that they had been diligent about setting up their affairs and had worked out all the details with Martin, their longtime attorney friend. In setting up the will, Martin assumed that both the husband and wife were US citizens. Unfortunately, that was not the case. Only Randy had full citizenship. Because Alysa had not applied for citizenship, she had a much higher tax

burden. This small but important detail created a lot of confusion and extra expense for the family. It is important to let your attorney and your CPA know about any beneficiaries who are not US citizens, so they can help you to explore the best options for estate planning.

☐ **Get advice on the recommended frequency of review of all relevant legal documents.** A common error is to assume a "once and done" approach. One pass through of the documents is not sufficient, and all the documents we have been discussing should be reviewed periodically. An attorney can provide the advice on the right time frame for reviewing your legal documents. You need regular reviews not only to take account of changes in your life (for instance, wanting to include a new grandchild in a will), but also to assess the plan as a whole. The more sophisticated the plan, the more likely a tax or legal change will affect it, and the more important the review process becomes.

☐ **Assess any special financial situations with regard to particular family members.** Get an attorney's advice on specific financial arrangements/agreements within the family and pay particular attention to anything that has not been recorded in writing. Clarify your wishes ahead of time. For example: Have all loans to family members been recorded? How will these be handled after death? Will they be forgiven? Will they be repaid by the individual to the estate? Is a beneficiary whose money management skills are poor better off with an income stream rather than a lump sum?

☐ **To aid with your preparations before you to meet with an attorney to officially draw up your legal documents, complete the "Estate Planning Items for Discussion" worksheet.** You will find it on the next page of this book.

Estate Planning Items for Discussion

Providing the following information can help your attorney develop an appropriate estate plan for You and your spouse or significant other.

1. **Who Will Make Financial Decisions?**

   Who will make financial decisions for you and your spouse? List the full names with middle initials, addresses, telephone numbers, and email addresses for your first and second choices.

   1. Name   _____
       Address   _____
       Telephone   _____
       City/State/Zip _____
       Email   _____

   2. Name   _____
       Address   _____
       Telephone   _____
       City/State/Zip _____
       Email   _____

2. **Who Will Make Medical Decisions?**

   Who will make medical decisions (including possibly end-of-life decisions)? List the full names with middle initials, addresses, telephone numbers, and email addresses for your first and second choices.

   1. **For**   2. **For**

   Name   _____   Name   _____
   Address   _____   Address   _____
   City/State/Zip _____   City/State/Zip _____
   Telephone   _____   Telephone   _____
   Email   _____   Email   _____

   1. **For**   2. **For**

   Name   _____   Name   _____
   Address   _____   Address   _____
   City/State/Zip _____   City/State/Zip _____
   Telephone   _____   Telephone   _____
   Email   _____   Email   _____

3. Who Should Inherit Your Property?

Who will inherit your property? List the percentage of your total estate rather than specific assets. Include the full name and relationship to each party.

Name_____Relationship_____% _____

Name_____Relationship_____% _____

Name_____Relationship_____% _____

4. If Your Heirs Predecease You

If any of your heirs predecease you, who should inherit their share of your estate? Name each heir and an alternate.

Heir _____   Alternate _____

Heir _____   Alternate _____

Heir _____   Alternate _____

5. Caring For Minor Children

If there are minor children, who will raise them if both parents are deceased? List the full name, address, telephone number, email address, and personal relationship for each guardian. List individuals rather than naming a couple.

Name   _____

Address   _____

City/State/Zip _____

Telephone   _____

Email   _____

Relationship _____

Name   _____

Address   _____

City/State/Zip _____

Telephone   _____

Email   _____

Relationship _____

6. At What Age Should Your Children or Young Adult Heirs Inherit Property?
This age may vary with the individual.

Name _____   Age to Inherit _____

Name _____   Age to Inherit _____

Name _____   Age to Inherit _____

Name _____   Age to Inherit _____

Name _____   Age to Inherit _____

Many people like to distribute a portion of the estate at several different times. For example, 1/3 at age 21, 1/3 at age 25 and 1/3 at age 30; or ½ at age 30 and ½ at age 35, etc.

If you want to influence either the timing of the inheritance or the way it gets spent, you'll need to use a trust.

This worksheet helped you prepare to get your legal documents completed or reviewed and revised. It did not legally bind any decisions. Furthermore, instructions in existing legal documents or newly created legal documents will override anything written here.

Tax Planning

You may decide that it makes sense to include an experienced Certified Public Accountant (CPA) in your inner circle. Here are the most important action items to discuss with a knowledgeable CPA who can help you manage your assets and obligations.

- ☐ **Make sure both state and federal tax returns are accurately filed and up to date.** If any tax returns are missing or incomplete, get the CPA's help in filing or updating the appropriate returns. Otherwise, your family will have an immense bureaucratic tangle to deal with when you pass away. In most cases where there is a backlog of multiple unfiled years, the IRS requires you to go back six years and file tax returns to get back in its good graces.

- ☐ **Make sure to discuss any gifting with your CPA.** If your financial plan has or will include gifting strategies, please make sure to discuss gift tax returns, which should be filed with your CPA.

Keep the IRS Happy

In our experience, it is not uncommon for people who experience illness or injury prior to death to (innocently) overlook or oversimplify their tax obligations. We have seen cases where five consecutive years of tax returns were not filed. The estate cannot be settled until this is taken care of. To avoid complex, time-consuming problems for your family and loved ones down the line, ask a CPA to assess your current tax status. Confirm that you have everything in order with regard to your personal tax obligations. You will save your loved ones a lot of trouble and aggravation (and penalty fees!) by doing this.

☐ **Clarify who will be responsible for filing your final tax return and introduce that person to your CPA.** Typically, this is the executor of the estate. It is important that this return be filed in a timely manner. The tax return filed on behalf of the deceased will be subject to the normal tax deadlines in the state where the person declared legal residence. The estate return is due within nine months of death.

☐ **Ask the CPA's advice on whether bequests should be made to specific beneficiaries or to a trust.** There can be major tax implications here. Disclose all relevant information for each beneficiary and get the CPA's feedback with regard to each one. This is a great opportunity to work collaboratively with your attorney and financial advisor so that all your advisors are on the same page. There are many unique planning tips that can avoid future taxation of your assets. One such creative planning technique is donating your retirement assets [IRAs or 401(k)s] to charities.

☐ **Have your CPA confirm the potential tax implications when the owner of a life insurance policy is not the insured.** If a trust, business, or spouse owns the policy, there is the potential for unexpected gift tax obligations. Ask your CPA and/or your insurance advisor for help in addressing this problem, which is often referred to as the "Goodman triangle." This issue commonly arises when one spouse takes out a policy on the other spouse and then names the children as beneficiaries, or when an adult child takes a policy out on one or both parents and names himself and his siblings as beneficiaries. This also happens when business owners are doing succession planning. Sometimes, ownership and beneficiary issues can be cleared up with a simple signature, but other times restructuring the policy is the best option. At the very least you should ask your CPA to bring you up to date on the potential tax implications for your beneficiaries so you can share that information with them.

☐ **Ask the CPA about the specific tax obligations and timelines your beneficiaries will face.** Nine months after death, the estate is expected to pay death tax obligations. Federal tax payments can be arranged on an installment plan, assuming the right person is identified and willing to pay the hefty interest charges, but state obligations are often more of a challenge because states tend to be less flexible in this regard. Identify the likely timelines and liquidity requirements your beneficiaries will face so that you can realistically address these needs with your financial advisors.

☐ **Ask for the CPA's estimate of the total tax obligations and probate costs the estate is likely to face.** This is typically underestimated, sometimes dramatically so. You do not want the estate placed in the position of having to sell family property—often at reduced prices—to make legally required tax and probate payments. Be knowledgeable upfront and avoid surprises later.

☐ **Ask for help in computing anticipated estate settlement costs and death taxes.** If you do not know what your state or federal death taxes are likely to be, you cannot plan for them. Work with your attorney, CPA, or financial advisor on what should and should not be included in the estate, and on other issues that will affect settlement costs and death tax obligations.

Being Proactive Pays Off

Many people believe that where taxes are concerned, they are victims, held hostage by an inevitable, impossible-to-understand process that allows them no input and no control over their situation. This passive thought process becomes something of a self-fulfilling prophecy. If you do not actively manage and challenge your advisors to work together for the best possible outcome for you and your family, you *will* lose control over your situation.

Financial Planning

The following to-do items are important for establishing a solid financial plan for your personal estate:

☐ **Identify and list all assets.** Review your asset list and get an attorney's help in evaluating the title status of all relevant properties.

☐ **Identify all advisors and introduce them to each other.** It is critically important that all advisors work collaboratively. Do not assume your financial advisor knows everything that needs to happen! The tax advisor (for instance) will be able to add important insights as well. Set up clear channels of communication when it comes to questions of administration and follow-through. The same principle applies to strategy discussions. If you are setting up a gifting or charitable strategy, you will want to be sure to coordinate your efforts with both the person who manages your investments *and* the person who does your taxes. You might create huge problems if your asset advisor does not know about the gifting strategy; alternatively, if you do not check in with your tax advisor, you might not think you can afford to make charitable gifts, when in fact you can. Your advisors need to work together to help you understand what you can feasibly do in terms of charitable giving, and which "buckets" are best left for someone to inherit. The larger lesson here is simple: If you are not willing to take on the responsibility of quarterbacking the game—and it is fine if you are not—make sure someone *is* there to take on that role and knows what to expect. Otherwise important to-do items will go unimplemented and important communication will not happen.

☐ **Select the right insurance advisor.** It is important to work with a professional insurance advisor who has a deep knowledge and expertise on insurance contracts. This person should be someone you trust. Select an advisor who is independent and has the resources to approach questions without bias to sit on your side of the table. If you already have a financial advisor who works with you comprehensively, he or she may be able to fulfill this role.

Alternatively, your financial advisor may have a strategic partner who can assist with the insurance questions.

☐ **Conduct an annual review of your insurance coverage.** When it comes to insurance, many people tend to think that as long as they have a policy in place and they keep paying their premiums each year, they will be fully covered in the event of an untimely death. Unfortunately, this may not the case. Personal situations change and coverages should be reviewed and updated annually. Too many families skip this step! You will want to meet with the insurance advisor to understand and analyze existing insurance coverage and revise the policies as necessary, based on current needs and future goals. Postponing this kind of regular review can lead to unnecessary problems.

Getting on the Same Page

Mary Ellen is a vibrant, independent widow who plays golf three days a week and is active in her retirement community. She is also very conscientious and has thoughtfully planned for her future if she is unable to live alone or needs extended medical assistance. She purchased a long-term care policy that will pay for home health care or nursing home care. Her plan is that her daughter, Leslie, will receive the long-term care benefit when she opts to move in with her because Leslie will be the one providing care. However, Leslie was not aware of her mother's wishes and plans until her advisor recommended a group family meeting. Leslie was able to discuss with her husband and confirm their desire to have Mary Ellen move in with them if she ever needs increased assistance. Leslie was also grateful and pleasantly surprised that her mother had taken steps for financial protection. This is something Leslie had secretly worried about, having seen her friends upheaved by a parent's sudden need for additional resources of both time and money. It is extremely important to schedule these regular meetings so you and your loved ones can share, review, and assess your goals for the future.

We cannot overemphasize the importance of working with a qualified insurance professional and conducting regular policy reviews with your family.

☐ **Think in terms of an "insurance portfolio," not in terms of "individual insurance policies."** Most people tend to think of their insurance plans as something that they set up once, check off a "to-do" list, and then do not need to re-examine. This is a major strategic error. Just as you must re-examine your financial portfolio to ensure that it is in line with your (possibly changing) goals over time and to adapt to changing economic circumstances, it is absolutely essential to schedule periodic reviews with an insurance professional to reassess your insurance portfolio, ask appropriate questions, make adjustments, and realign the policies with your current situation.

☐ **Disclose all relevant information to your insurance advisor.** Make sure you and your advisor are aware of the entire scope of your planning. Do not overlook anything! Your insurance advisor is an important member of your team and needs to know all the details. If your advisor does not ask good questions, it is because they do not know enough about your personal situation. It could also be because they have predetermined what you will be "buying." The right advisor will not "sell you" but rather will consult, ask lots of questions, listen to learn about your needs, and review your entire estate and goals before making a recommendation.

☐ **Ask your insurance advisor to request an *in-force illustration* specifying exactly what will happen with your current policy/ policies.** Assumptions change, goals change, and the economy changes. This means you need more than just a snapshot of what will happen on a certain date; you need a motion picture that shows the larger trends. That is what an in-force illustration will provide you. An insurance advisor will not only secure this for you but will also walk you through it and help you to understand what it means.

Making the Most of Your Insurance Portfolio

Statistically, the average insurance consumer will modify their life insurance portfolio seven times over the course of a lifetime. Someone may buy their first policy when they get married and then upgrade it upon the birth of a child. They may start off purchasing term insurance and then move to an interest-sensitive whole life policy. The type and performance of life insurance policies selected can be expected to change often. With the general population living longer, internal mortality costs on life insurance policies have gone down. This means that older insurance contracts need to be reviewed often because it is possible that the consumer purchased an insurance policy that was aligned with rates during a high interest rate and mortality cost environment. When the rates dropped, the insurance company lowered the interest rates accordingly, but the consumer did not realize this could happen until many years later, when they were notified they had to either pay a higher premium to keep the same death benefit or choose a lower death benefit. This is yet another reason to schedule regular reviews with a qualified insurance professional who can "translate" the terms of your policy and help you make good decisions going forward.

☐ **Ask your insurance advisor to explain the various contract features.** You need to know exactly what the landscape looks like when it comes to the actual life insurance contract. There are many special features such as accelerated death benefit options, vitality and wellness discounts, waiver of premiums in the event of a disability, critical illness riders, and other beneficial provisions that may allow you to deal with special circumstances.

Who Knew?

Bill was diagnosed with amyotrophic lateral sclerosis (ALS, or Lou Gehrig's disease) when he was 57 years old. ALS is a progressive disease that attacks the nervous system and eventually leaves the person totally disabled. With this diagnosis, Bill became uninsurable and was unable to purchase additional life insurance. His immediate focus was on maintaining what coverage he already had so that he could preserve and extend some benefit to his wife and children. When Bill reviewed his current policies with his insurance professional, he learned that his policy had an important, previously overlooked feature: a waiver of the premium provision in the event of disability. As a result of this discovery, he was able to convert his term insurance to a permanent policy without going through the medical underwriting process, a major advantage to both Bill and his family.

Bill discovered this feature in his existing policy only because he had worked closely with his advisor, purchased the right benefit, and scheduled the time for a regular review of his insurance portfolio.

☐ **Know the difference between term and permanent.** Term insurance is often purchased to provide death benefit coverage for a specified period of time (10, 15, 20, or 30 years) with level premiums and a level death benefit. Permanent insurance is often purchased to provide coverage for a lifetime, or permanently, so you have death benefit for your entire life and you hope a claim will pay out to beneficiaries far in the future. Find out which kind of insurance you have and discuss the best current options with your insurance advisor. It is extremely important to understand what kind of policies are in place, what the objectives were when they were purchased, and what the objectives are now. You may be able to convert a policy from one category to another to meet a current objective.

☐ **Select the right investment advisor.** You may work with an advisor who works comprehensively with all of your accounts, insurance, and investments, including retirement. Or, this person could be a member of your team. As mentioned earlier, it is important to get members of your team on the same page as you develop a clearer picture of your goals and objectives.

☐ **What will happen to your accounts when you die?** It is all too common for an investment account to have no named beneficiary. That means it will have to pass through probate, and even if the money eventually gets into the right hands after probate, your intended beneficiaries might lose out on opportunities to make important decisions that affect their tax obligations.

☐ **Discuss "stretch provisions" with your investment advisor, financial planner, or CPA.** If you have an IRA, 401(k), or other qualified account, your beneficiary has options to stretch that inherited money out over time. It is important to make sure you understand these options, so you don't inadvertently disqualify your intended beneficiary from receiving the money in a tax-efficient way.

A Teachable Moment

During a routine review of accounts, Joe mentioned to his advisor that a colleague had just inherited some money and his colleague mentioned "stretching the payments." Joe's colleague told him that he had to take money out of the account every year and scheduled the withdrawal for around the holidays, but that he didn't have to take it all and thus "avoided one large, lump-sum tax." His advisor explained that his colleague was likely a beneficiary of a qualified account, a 401(k) or Individual Retirement Account (IRA) who decided to use "stretch provisions." Joe asked whether his children would be able to stretch out the money they would receive if he died. The investment advisor pulled up the accounts and noticed that on one annuity, the beneficiary was Joe's Revocable Trust. The advisor explained that a trust had different "stretch" options and would likely have to distribute all the money within five years of Joe's death, based on IRS guidelines. However, if Joe wanted to, he could name his children directly as beneficiaries so they would have the option to stretch the account over their lifetimes. Joe couldn't remember why he named the revocable trust as beneficiary but thought maybe it was to avoid probate or because at the time his children were minors. Joe's advisor assured him that naming his now older children as beneficiaries directly would still avoid probate. The advisor explained that there can be other reasons to name the trust as beneficiary, including the potential for more control. With this information, Joe was able to speak to his attorney and advisor and make a better decision about how he wanted to name the beneficiary of his largest account.

☐ **Not all accounts are worth the same at death.** By this we mean that all accounts are inherited differently from the perspective of taxes and step-up in basis (the readjustment of the value of an appreciated asset for tax purposes upon inheritance, determined to be the higher market value of the asset at the time of inheritance). Ask your advisor to explain which accounts receive a step-up in basis at your death. An example would be someone with $750,000 who wants to distribute those funds equally to a charity, a child, and a grandchild. If that person has $250,000 in a qualified account (an IRA), $250,000 in life insurance death benefit, and $250,000 in a nonqualified stocks and bonds account, there is a tax-efficient way to name the beneficiaries and an inefficient way.

Charitable Giving

There are many charitable giving strategies that allow you to contribute to your favorite cause while retaining an income stream and protecting your estate. If you are charitably inclined and have prioritized giving to be part of your legacy, you should speak with your trusted team of advisors and ask for their help in making the best decision for you and your family. Charitable giving can be done in many ways, such as through a separate foundation, a donor-advised fund, or as a direct gift from one of your investments. It is important to collaborate with your professional advisors to appropriately address your charitable giving desires, so that you stay on the right side of the law, choose the best account from which to donate, and maximize your tax benefits.

Charitable giving is most effective and sustainable when it is connected to what matters to you the most. Some common areas of interest include the following:

- Spiritual or religious institutions

- A specific cause, such as youth sports, homelessness, or

cancer research

- Educational institutions

- A desire to share your good fortune with others

☐ **If you plan to use a significant portion of your estate to support a charitable cause, discuss this decision with your family, and base your choice on a clearly defined mission that others will understand—and be able to support.** The bigger the gift, the more important it is to align the funds with a clearly defined mission that arises out of something that your family will understand is personally important to you. For example, donating a significant portion of your estate to a local public television station you recently discovered may or may not make sense to family members who had no idea the station was important to you. Donating the same funds to a wildlife protection organization may be easier for them to accept if they already know of, respect, and accept your lifelong love of the outdoors and know that the mission of protecting wildlife has been a passion of yours for decades.

☐ **Choose the right people.** You need a good team to manage your donor-advised fund or charitable foundation. If you are setting up a foundation devoted to a specific charitable cause and you have any doubts about the commitment of people in your family to follow through on your vision, make sure you express your wishes in writing about how you expect the foundation will support specific bequests and causes.

☐ **Beware of "checkbook philanthropy."** Be specific with your bequests; do not ask your heirs to guess which worthwhile cause you would support. If there is a cause you are passionate about, make your preference known. Be as clear as you possibly can; try to align your philanthropic bequests with a well-defined mission, ideally one that your family and loved ones can embrace and support.

Bringing Clarity to the Charitable Vision

Melanie worked with her attorney to make a major change in her estate planning. She and her husband had set up a family foundation and wanted oversight to pass to their second son instead of his older brother. Melanie and her husband's philanthropic focus differed from those of some of their children, especially their oldest son, and they wanted to make sure the family foundation's resources were not pointed in directions they did not approve of!

Unfortunately, they made this change without telling their sons, which was a perfect recipe for conflict and resentment. It is almost impossible to imagine a scenario when one or more adult children would not feel hurt or excluded by such a decision. They might have made matters a little easier for all concerned if they had chosen a nonfamily member with a relevant professional background to lead the foundation and, most importantly, had shared that information with the family.

There are any number of situations when it may make sense to direct some assets toward a particular charitable goal. Some people approach this part of estate planning with the goal of securing a tax advantage; others consider this path because of firmly held personal beliefs and experiences; still others feel that the option of giving the resources to a charitable cause is the most responsible course of action for the family as a whole. Whichever path you choose, be sure to talk to a qualified professional about the legal and tax implications.

Life Changes

We have made suggestions at various points about how often you should review and update important documents, but we would like to emphasize here how important it is to make these updates whenever you experience a major life event that will affect your priorities, such as marriage, divorce, the birth of a child or grandchild, or a change in health for you or your beneficiary. When important events in your life happen, take action! Update your documents to reflect these new circumstances and make it a priority *right now.* Your friends and loved ones will be grateful you did!

Titling and Beneficiaries

Jane, a well-respected professor, passed away at a young age after a courageous battle with cancer. She was an inspiration to many, most of all her husband, Bob, and her sister, Susan. After many months of grieving, celebrating Jane's life, and continuing to bring awareness to Jane's most precious cause, cancer research, Bob and Susan were still working to settle her estate. One of the accounts Jane had was an IRA on which her sister Susan was named as beneficiary. Susan and Bob both thought everything had been retitled to Bob, so they were surprised to see that this account worth more than $100,000 had to be claimed by Susan or it would go to the estate and through probate. Susan decided to take over the account and then give Bob the funds, and together they decided they would make a donation to Jane's favorite charity. It wasn't until Susan completed her tax return that she realized that she was liable for paying the taxes on the entire account, which she had given in full to Bob.

Bob worked with Susan to pay the taxes owed and discussed the charitable deduction with his accountant to make sure everyone was treated fairly. Bob felt horrible about the hassle Jane's sister had to go through, especially considering she had been so generous in doing what her sister would have wanted.

Section IV:
Personal Wishes

Take the Pressure Off Your Loved Ones

By planning ahead and sharing your final wishes about funeral and/or memorial arrangements, you will take the pressure off your family.

Maria was the oldest sibling and the most financially secure member of her family. When Maria's mother, Tara, died, she left no instructions about the kind of funeral service she wanted. As the oldest and "most successful," Maria took on the task of coordinating Tara's funeral arrangements—it was what her siblings expected of her. They also expected her to pay the entire cost by herself. Maria ended up paying over $16,000 for a funeral service that she knew her mother probably would not have selected. Why? Maria did not want to "look cheap" to her less-well-off siblings. She felt strongly that her mother would have preferred a simpler memorial ceremony and cremation, but because she had no written instructions, Maria succumbed to peer pressure to plan a formal funeral. She could have had a much easier time had her mother simply taken the time to write down her wishes, put them in a safe place, and let someone else know about them.

One of the most powerful gifts you can give your loved ones is to let them know what your wishes are for the period immediately following your death. Whether death comes suddenly or is anticipated after a long illness, it brings a tidal wave of emotions for those who are grieving. Numerous decisions need to be made quickly during this emotional time. Anything you can do in advance to make this traumatic period easier for the family is worth considering.

Funeral Planning

Discussions about funeral arrangements usually occur quickly after a death and having to make decisions can be daunting for your loved ones. You can simplify the job by making a thorough checklist to make sure you have not only taken care of every important aspect of planning the funeral but have also discussed these issues appropriately and sensitively with those most concerned.

☐ **Select the person who should oversee the funeral arrangements.** Connect with this person ahead of time and share your specific wishes.

☐ **Complete the "Funeral Planning" worksheet.** This brief document will lay out what you want the service to look like. Complete and make copies of the form on next page and share with your family or the person you have tasked with planning your funeral.

Funeral Planning

Planning your own funeral or memorial service can provide priceless peace-of-mind to you and your family.

Your wishes for your body:

- ❑ **Cremation**
    - ❑ Before funeral
    - ❑ After funeral
    - ❑ Disbursement of ashes _____

- ❑ **Burial**
    Type of property
    - ❑ Mausoleum   ❑ Ground burial   ❑ Lawn crypt   ❑ Urn/Niche
    - ❑ Legal description (if known)   _____
    - ❑ Type of memorial/marker   _____
    - ❑ Is there an inscription/epitaph you would like _____
    - ❑ Mortuary/funeral home/cemetery
        Name _____
        Address _____
        Phone number _____

    Have you prepaid for any funeral services? ❑ Yes ❑ No

    I have the right to be buried in a military cemetery
    ❑ Yes ❑ No

    I have a deceased
    ❑ Spouse ❑ Parent ❑ Child who is buried at _____

    I wish to be buried next to such person _____

Casket Preferences

- ❑ Least expensive   ❑ Midrange   ❑ Elaborate   ❑ I have prepaid

Do you want a "visitation" prior to the funeral service?
❑ Yes ❑ No

Do you want the casket open for viewing?
❑ Yes ❑ No

If yes, by whom?
❑ Family only   ❑ Everyone   ❑ Selected people only

Donate Your Body or Organs for Medical Study

☐   No

☐   Yes, arrangements have been made

☐   Yes, please make appropriate arrangements

Prayers, Poems, Readings

I would like the following people to deliver prayers or other readings:

1. _____

2. _____

3. _____

The readings I would like them to deliver are _____

Title _____   Author/Source _____

Songs/Music

I would like the following songs, hymns, or pieces of music to be played:

1. _____

2. _____

3. _____

Flowers/Donations

I would prefer the following types of flowers: _____

Would you like donations in lieu of flowers?

☐ Yes ☐ No

If so, list details here:

Service

What type of service do you want to have?

    Location:

    I would like my funeral or memorial service to be held at the following location: _____

    If this location is not available, my second choice is _____

    I have papers on file at: _____

Officiant

I would like the following person to officiate at my funeral or memorial service: _____

If this person is not available, my second choice is: _____

Pallbearers

I would like the following people to serve as pallbearers:
1.
2.
3.
4.
5.
6.

I would like the following people to serve as honorary pallbearers:

1.
2.

Eulogies

I would like the following people to deliver eulogies:

1.
2.

Special Notifications

Are there any groups, organizations, and clubs (veteran's groups, alumni associations, sports or hobby clubs, etc.) you would like to be notified of and invited to your funeral or memorial service?

Name of Group/Primary Contact_____

Contact Information _____

Please be sure the following people are notified of and invited to my funeral or memorial service

Name_____   Contact Information _____

Name_____   Contact Information _____

Name_____   Contact Information _____

Other Special Requests

Are there specific clothes you would like to be buried in or is there specific jewelry you would like to wear?

Military flag given to (if applicable) _____

Obituary

Please publish my obituary
❑ Yes   ❑   No

I have already drafted an obituary. ❑   Yes (Location_____) ❑ No

If I have not drafted an obituary, please prepare one using the following information and instructions below.

Obituary Overview
    Length: ❑   Brief   ❑   Moderate   ❑   Article Length
    Photograph: ❑   Yes   (Location_____) ❑ No
    Publications:

Obituary Details
    Date and place of birth
    Military service
    Spouse, children, grandchildren, parents, siblings
    Employment and business interests
    Memberships and committees
    Education
    Awards and achievements
    Interests and hobbies
    Values

Public or Private

My wishes for public or private ceremonies
    ❑ Viewing, visitation, or wake
    ❑ Funeral or memorial service
    ❑ Reception or celebration of life

Flowers
    ❑ Yes
    ❑ No. "No flowers, please."
    ❑ No. In lieu of flowers, please send donations to [list organization(s)].

Lastly, make sure your loved ones know your wishes. Share this worksheet with them and make sure to keep a copy with your other important documents.

☐ **State your preferences concerning cremation, body donation, organ donation, and/or natural burial.** There is no one "right" answer here, but it is worth noting that some funeral homes will *not* make a point of emphasizing the significant differences in costs between cremation and burial. If you do not want the family to incur any unnecessary expense and you prefer cremation, make sure to put that in writing. In the absence of such clearly stated wishes, many families find themselves agreeing to expensive funeral plans because they believe that is what their deceased loved one wanted.

☐ **Share your preferences for the final service.** If you prefer a traditional funeral, you can make the family's experience easier by choosing the funeral home, the casket, the pallbearers, the type of service, the burial spot, and the grave marker and/or inscription. If you want a religious service, now is the time to specify that, and to specify any readings that should be incorporated. If you want a particular individual to speak at the service or have any preference regarding music, make that clear as well.

☐ **Prepaid funeral plans.** Insurance companies and funeral homes often tout the advantages of prepaid funeral plans to spare the survivors trouble and expense, lock in current prices, and/or shelter assets from Medicaid. You should interview and evaluate multiple funeral homes before signing any agreement. There are some potential drawbacks that you should be aware of if you decide to prepay your funeral costs, among them misunderstood contracts and unforeseen additional fees. A more common approach is to prearrange your funeral without prepaying. You still do all the planning and share that with your family, giving them the peace of mind in knowing that important decisions have been made and thoughtfully discussed.

☐ **Get an estimate of the total funeral costs.** Depending on your family, cultural, or religious traditions, you may prefer a large-scale funeral service, a simple celebration of life, or something in between. According to the American Association of Retired Persons (AARP), the average funeral cost in 2018 was $8,500, which includes embalming, a viewing, burial, hearse, transfer of remains, and local services fees. With additional expenses, such as flowers and a luncheon afterwards, experts recommend you put aside $20,000 if you plan a more traditional funeral with all services to be included. It is prudent to get estimates from several funeral homes in advance. It makes sense to look at all the numbers carefully, and to make these decisions well ahead of time, rather than simply assuming the estate will have sufficient funds to cover all your wishes. Understand that the money the estate spends on an expensive funeral is money that *won't* be passed along to family members and/or others. In some instances, the estate does not have funds readily available to pay for services so quickly and the responsibility for the funeral falls to family members who must dip into their own accounts.

☐ **If you want a "simple" memorial service, write down your specific preferences.** Bear in mind that there is the potential for conflict within the family if you do not specify your wishes in writing.

☐ **Consider writing an obituary in advance.** Writing an obituary can be a daunting task, but your loved ones will appreciate an advance draft of what you would like in your obituary. At the most basic level, the obituary serves as a notice in the local newspaper of the death and the specifics of the funeral plans. An obituary is also a chance to celebrate and share one's life and acknowledge important family members. In addition, consider that this is the medium by which most people will learn of your wishes regarding final funeral arrangements and whether memorial donations are preferred in lieu of flowers.

☐ **Arrange for a visual tribute.** As funerals become increasingly personalized and unique, more and more families are creating visual memory tributes—a collection of pictures, memorabilia, and personal treasures placed on display in the funeral home for guests to view and appreciate. This tribute can also serve as a keepsake for family members to view at a later time.

Other Important Expressions of Your Wishes

If you are responsible for any dependents, it is important that you leave instructions clarifying how they will receive care following your death. Dependents may include children, elderly parents or relatives under your care, pets, and any loved ones who require your assistance with day-to-day tasks.

To ensure that your dependents receive the best care possible, you should include your preferences in a memo that can be made available to whomever you have settled on and confirmed legally as the guardian.

Consider sharing your preferences on the following matters for dependents other than pets:

- Education

- Religion

- Housing

- How you would like to see the inheritance monies spent/allocated

Even if there are no dependents to consider, you may opt to leave a special message for loved ones to reflect upon. Some people choose to leave a personal letter in which they write down what they wish to see for their loved ones' futures.

In composing such a letter, think of how you would want your loved ones to remember you. Offer advice on lessons learned, values cherished, and aspirations for the future. You may want to share an overarching message about what you have learned about love, kindness, and laughter; you may choose to share your wishes for how they should carry on in your memory. You can even include special memories you want to be sure are passed on to the next generation. Consider using upbeat phrases such as, "In this beautiful life, I have learned the value of family time, and I hope that after my passing, you continue to gather often, share smiles, and spread love like wildfire." Keep your message happy and upbeat. Above all, make sure what you write comes from the heart. This message should truly reflect who you are and what you want for those you love.

- ☐ **Consider writing an ethical will (also known as a love letter).** This is a nonbinding document that includes elements such as your personal and spiritual values, hopes, dreams, life experiences, love, blessings, and forgiveness.

- ☐ **Consider composing a memorandum of wishes.** This is a simple document that assigns possession of items of small financial value that you choose not to include on your formal asset inventory. This vehicle is appropriate for objects that hold primarily sentimental value, such as a ring that you consider a family heirloom or a sports trophy you won in college. You can use the memorandum of wishes to dispose of property that did not seem appropriate to give to an individual. For instance, if all your children already have reliable cars, you could use a memorandum of wishes to donate your automobile to a charity.

  - o **Consider requesting a memorial contribution in lieu of flowers.** At a time of loss, people express sympathy in various ways. They may choose to attend the wake or funeral, prepare a meal for the family, take care of children or pets, watch your home, send flowers, or contribute to a charity. If you want to channel memorial donations to a particular charity, that can be indicated in the obituary. Often, you will see suggestions like the following in an obituary:

  - o Memorial contributions may be made to …

  - o As an expression of sympathy, memorial contributions may be sent to …

  - o Remembrances may be made to the following charity:

  - o The family suggest memorial contributions may be sent to …

  - o In lieu of flowers, the family requests that donations be sent to …

If Death Is Imminent

Facing the imminent death of a loved one is stressful for the caregiver and also serves as a reminder that time is very precious. If you are providing end-of-life care for a loved one, there are many things you can do to help the person attend to unfinished business, and make things easier for the family by suggesting, tactfully, that certain basic preparatory steps be taken. These include the following:

- ☐ **Confirm the location of important items.** Specifically, confirm the location of the person's will, birth certificate, Social Security information, marriage and divorce certificates, life insurance policies, relevant financial documents, and the keys to the person's safety deposit box and/or home safe. On a related note, always make sure someone has copies of the house keys and car keys.

- ☐ **Confirm the person's wishes regarding organ donation, funeral arrangements, and burial or cremation.** This will save the person's loved ones a lot of guesswork.

- ☐ **Confirm that an advance healthcare directive is in place** so the family is aware of the person's wishes regarding the care the person does or *does not* wish to receive in certain circumstances.

- ☐ **Confirm that a healthcare proxy is in place** to allow the identified person to make important medical decisions if the patient becomes incapacitated.

- ☐ **If a do-not-resuscitate (DNR) order is in place, ensure it is highly visible.** This document tells healthcare professionals not to perform cardiopulmonary resuscitation if the patient's heart or breathing stops and a functional life would not be possible in the event of his or her revival. A DNR order might be part of a hospice plan if the patient is admitted to a hospital. The focus of care with a DNR is not to prolong life, but to treat symptoms of pain or shortness of breath and to maintain comfort.

- ☐ **Share notarized copies of all legal documents** with the patient's selected family members and friends, and make sure they are easily accessible if they are needed.

☐ **Provide notarized copies of important healthcare documents to the hospital** if the loved one is admitted there, or to the hospice or caretaker location.

> ### End-of-Life Planning: A Blessing
>
> When Nancy's mother passed away at 93 under hospice care, the nurse knew who to call and what to do, so the death and its immediate aftermath were, in Nancy's words, "peaceful and seamless." Nancy's mother had discussed end-of-life arrangements with Nancy and her three sisters, the hospice nurse, and the hospice counselor. Since all the right legal documents, list of medications, medical records, and who to call were there, they were able to be fully present with their mother rather than logistics. She died with dignity, surrounded by her three loving daughters.

The Greatest Gift You Give

Most people learn about end-of-life planning and closing out an estate the hard way—when death actually occurs. Planning for death is just as important as planning for life. We plan most major events in life—weddings, births, vacations, and retirement—yet most people fail to plan for death. You may ask yourself, why does it really matter? It matters because:

- It will allow your loved ones to grieve knowing they have clear instructions on what to do next.

- It will eliminate guesswork and save your family time, stress, and money.

- It will assure that your wishes will be honored.

Like planning for life, planning for death can be the greatest gift a person can give or receive.

Part Two:
After a Loved One Has Died

Gaining Confidence: Caring for Yourself and Others … and Upholding Your Loved One's Wishes

The death of a loved one is an emotional hurricane, the kind of total disruption for which you can never properly prepare, even when there are clear signs long in advance of what is about to happen. When you lose someone close to you, you will likely experience an unpredictable period of stress, depression, and anxiety that can be both overwhelming and debilitating.

It is during this period of upheaval that we are both our strongest and most fragile as human beings. At the same time, we are faced with critical decisions and must take on important responsibilities in a very short time frame.

This part of the guidebook will provide direction on what needs to happen immediately after the death of a loved one and give you confidence that you are not missing a critical step in executing your loved one's final wishes and settling the estate. For decisions that are less logistical (administrative) in nature, we also provide some discussion points to facilitate meaningful conversations that will instill confidence that you have acted in alignment with the wishes of your loved one.

We have seen many families endure needless crisis, delay, dysfunction, expense, and estrangement, all arising from poor or ill-advised decisions, and from a lack of proper counsel and guidance during this period. With those families in mind, we believe two essential pieces of advice are particularly relevant here.

First and foremost, during this uniquely challenging period, make a point of taking care of yourself, both physically and emotionally. In order to make the clearest decisions and maintain your own health, try to avoid drastically altering your daily habits such as eating properly and getting exercise. Allow yourself to freely give and receive emotional support from others in your inner circle. Do not attempt to assume all the responsibility—managing the closure of an estate is a collaborative undertaking, and no individual can do it alone. It is an ongoing and often complicated process. Consider the advice a flight attendant offers passengers before a plane takes off: In case of emergency, put on your own oxygen mask before attempting to help someone else.

Second, pace yourself. Do not try to do everything at once. Do a little bit each day, and bear in mind that the process of squaring everything away is likely to take between 9 and 12 months, depending on the complexity of the estate. Many of the steps involve other parties and their timelines for completion, so you should not expect to complete everything quickly. Use the next part of this book to help prioritize what must get done immediately. Take care of those items first, and work through the remaining steps as you move forward.

Immediate Action Steps

Take the following steps as soon as possible:

- [ ] **If the loved one died at home without hospice care, call 911 to report the death.** If the loved one died at home under hospice care, contact the hospice nurse, who can make a formal declaration of death and can help you arrange for transport of the body.

- [ ] **If there is a do-not-resuscitate order (DNR), be ready to present it.** If a do-not-resuscitate document exists, you will want to show it to the paramedics when they arrive. Without this document, paramedics are obligated to start and continue emergency procedures unless you are in a jurisdiction where they are legally authorized to pronounce death or take the loved one to an emergency room so that a physician can make an official declaration of death.

- [ ] **Identify the loved one's instructions concerning organ donation or donation of his or her body to science.** If the loved one was an organ donor and wished to donate body parts and/or tissues to a medical institution, or wished to donate his or her entire body, and you have documentation of this, discuss the next steps with the doctor, coroner, or hospice worker. Check the loved one's driver's license or final instructions for guidance here and pass the relevant information on to the right medical care professional as soon as possible.

☐ **Make sure the death is recorded.** Depending on the manner of death, this may mean reaching out to a doctor (assuming a doctor was not present at the time of death) and obtaining a death certificate. The ideal person to call is a physician who is familiar with the loved one's case. If you don't know who the physician is, call 911 to report the death.

☐ **Call the members of the loved one's immediate family.** Inform them of the death tactfully and directly. Ask for help with this difficult task if you need it. Bear in mind that the potential for hurt feelings is significant if someone receives word later than he or she expects to and think twice before posting the news on social media.

☐ **Arrange for transportation of the body.** If you are working with a funeral home, they will take care of this step for you. Ask the funeral home for a quote over the phone for all services provided, including transporting the body. If the funeral home refuses to provide a quote, call a different funeral home. (Note: Most states do not require that you work with a licensed funeral director to transport a body, but some do, so you are advised to secure the services of a funeral home or other licensed institution, such a mortuary or crematorium, or call the local coroner's office for help and advice in dealing with your situation.)

☐ **If the deceased had children arrange for their care.** Every child reacts differently to learning that a loved one has died. Some children cry. Some ask questions. Others seem not to react at all. The most important thing is to be present and respond to emotions with compassion and understanding. The grieving process takes time, so you need to make sure the child is safe, comforted, and well taken care of.

☐ **Arrangements may need to be made for care of elderly parents of the deceased.** If the decedent took care of their parents, do your best to determine what they did to help and coordinate efforts so you can be sure that support remains in effect. Focus on the most immediate concerns first, but bear in mind as well that the decedent may have helped their parents financially, with paying bills, or even coordinating schedules for doctors visits.

☐ **If the deceased had any pets, arrange care for them.** This task is often overlooked. Visit the deceased's home as soon as possible and check on the condition of any animals. Do not leave them unattended. Find a safe place for them, even if it is only temporary. The estate can pay expenses related to pets, just as it can for dependents. Keep good records and save all receipts.

☐ **Secure and take care of the deceased's home and property.** Put valuables such as cash, jewelry, and collectible items in a safe place. Be sure the house is locked when no one is home. Make sure neighbors are aware of the person's passing so they can also watch the property. Set up a "lights on" schedule for the house as part of your home security planning.

☐ **Identify the loved one's instructions concerning preferences for his or her funeral and burial arrangements.** If there are no instructions, consult with the family about what the right next step is.

   o **Look for a "Letter of Instruction," "Final Instructions," or "Disposition Authorization"** for information on wishes regarding funeral or memorial services arrangements, and burial or cremation arrangements.

   o **Note that "Designated Agent" instructions about who is to take care of those arrangements are sometimes included in advance directive documents,** such as in a durable power of attorney for health care or a living will. If you have trouble locating these or other important documents, ask the deceased's close friends and/or attorney for help in finding them.

   o **Look for information on any preplanned funeral arrangements that the deceased may have made,** such as burial or cremation. On a similar note, look for funeral insurance documents.

o **Determine whether the loved one belonged to or was affiliated with a memorial society that can help make special burial or memorial arrangements.** Examples include a military or police honor guard.

☐ **Consider holding an initial meeting to set priorities and determine responsibilities.** It is all too easy to jump into action mode at times of high stress, but before you act, you should probably have a planning session with all the key people, both inside and outside the family. Complex estates will also require input from the family's trusted professional advisors. Use this session to create a single objective for the estate management process, one that everyone agrees on, and then circulate that objective in writing after the meeting. Two examples of such an objective would be "Maximize the value of the estate" and "Get this over with as soon as we can." Note that if you are the executor—the person who is legally responsible for carrying out the deceased's wishes as outlined in the will and settling the estate—you would not be able to pursue both objectives at the same time because these two goals are mutually exclusive. Yet it is possible, and indeed likely, that people in your inner circle will have very different ideas about what your primary objective as executor should be. You and your key people will need to identify *one* driving objective for the estate and agree on it. If you cannot do that during this initial meeting, you should try to at least introduce the topic of selecting a single objective and get consensus on the importance of identifying one and only one driving goal. If you enter this process with no clear, agreed-upon outcome in mind, you will have a very difficult time fulfilling your responsibilities as executor. All your priorities as executor should align with the mutually agreed-upon outcome you are pursuing!

☐ **Call the deceased's employer.** Make sure the employer knows what has happened; get as much information as you can about final paychecks, benefit plans, and insurance and retirement benefits. Keep detailed records and write everything down.

☐ **Keep track of the important documents you are able to secure.** Locate critical documents, inventory them with a summary list, and keep them in a safe place.

☐ **Choose the disposition.** "Disposition" means what happens to the deceased's remains. This is a potentially emotional issue. We have seen plenty of situations when a family member "inherits" the task of organizing funeral or memorial service arrangements and, under pressure to make decisions quickly, neglects to include people in the discussion who should have been included. This is usually an honest oversight that takes place under the intense pressure of wanting to finalize the arrangements within the first 48 to 72 hours after death. A particularly common scenario is reaching out to your own close family members for their opinions, but not extending the same courtesy to your in-laws. These kinds of mistakes can cause long-lasting resentments and may even end some relationships! If you suddenly find yourself "in charge" of disposition, be sure to reach out and consult *all* the people the loved one would have wanted you to consult.

Funeral Arrangements

If you are making arrangements for a loved one who left no instructions about the kind of service he or she had in mind, consider the following questions:

☐ **What kind of service do you have in mind?** Popular choices include a traditional funeral with a viewing and an indoor funeral service, followed by cemetery burial; a memorial service with cremated remains or without the deceased being present; or a graveside service held at the cemetery.

☐ **What city or town do you want the service take place in?**

☐ **Is there an existing family plot? If so, where is the deed?**

☐ **Does a burial make the most sense?**

    o **If a burial makes sense, should you look for a funeral home that operates its own cemetery, or is there a** cemetery with a burial location elsewhere that you should consider?

☐ **What clothing or personal items should be selected for the viewing/burial?**

☐ **Does cremation make the most sense?**

  o **If cremation makes the most sense, should you look for a funeral home that operates its own crematorium?**

☐ **Alternatively, should you look for a cremation provider that does not operate as part of a funeral home (a potentially less expensive option)?** For help finding the latter, visit https://www.cremationassociation.org/.

☐ **Do you want to select a funeral home with a particular cultural or religious affiliation?**

☐ **How should you check the reputation of the funeral home that you are considering using?** Good options here include getting feedback from family, friends, and members of your community and/or looking at online reviews.

☐ **Should you schedule an in-person consultation?** This is particularly important and highly recommended if you are considering using a funeral home.

Additional considerations for planning final services are below:

☐ **The funeral home can help write the obituary for any newspaper or internet submission.** They will likely ask you to provide place of residence; name of spouse, children, and children's spouses and residence; grandchildren, siblings, and any other significant person that would need to be mentioned (partner, godchildren, nieces, or nephews). You may want to include predeceased family members. You may also want to include a picture.

☐ **Arrange for the death certificate to be completed.** A funeral home will prepare the death certificate and will walk you through a fact-gathering session with information such as marital status at time of death, maiden name (if applicable), place of birth, date of birth, Social Security number, and parents' names and where they were born.

☐ **Consider requesting multiple copies of the death certificate.** You will need these for forthcoming discussions with government agencies, financial institutions, and insurers. Note that each certified copy of the death certificate is likely to require a fee; some institutions will accept photocopies or scans of a death certificate; others will not.

☐ **Be aware of important information and items you need to gather.** Specifically, you should have access to originals and/or copies of the following items:

    o   Deceased's military discharge papers (if applicable)

    o   Birth certificate

    o   Documents related to prepaid gravestone, plot, or other arrangements

About the Death Certificate

The death certificate, which is issued by local authorities, serves as formal confirmation that a person has died. This certificate is essential for a number of estate purposes, specifically claiming life insurance benefits, transferring titles, claiming Social Security survivor benefits, and closing bank and investment accounts. You will likely need multiple copies of this certificate. Most funeral homes will request copies of the death certificate on the family's behalf.

Death certificates are kept on file either in your state's vital statistics or vital records office, or in a city or county office, such as the health department or county recorder's office. If you are uncertain about how to obtain a death certificate, contact city hall or your town's municipal offices and ask for guidance.

The following information will be required when you apply for a copy of a death certificate:

    o   Month, day, and year of birth

o   Month, day, and year of death

o   Place of birth

o   Place of death

o   Full name of the deceased person whose record is being requested

o   Gender of the deceased

o   Parents' names, including mother's maiden name

o   Reason for requesting copies of the death certificate

o   Applicant's relationship to the deceased

Cremation Is an Increasingly Popular Choice

If your loved one expressed no preference about how his or her final remains should be handled, it makes sense to consider cremation. Roughly half of all families arranging final ceremonies for a loved one now opt for cremation over traditional burial services, which represents a significant increase over previous decades. There is a significant cost advantage to approaching the final arrangements in this way: The process is often seen as the most appropriate for a loved one who had a strong connection to a spot in nature, such as a beloved forest, golf course, beach, or stretch of open sea. Scattering the loved one's ashes in such a location may be appropriate in your situation. Discuss this option with the family members to determine whether cremation makes sense for your loved one.

☐   **Arrange for help with the funeral.** Assign key tasks such as designing the funeral program (if there is to be one), cooking, shopping, caring for children, caring for pets, and acting as pallbearer.

☐   **If there is to be a headstone, arrange for that.** You may opt to secure a headstone through the cemetery you choose, or by working with an outside vendor. Be sure to confirm the necessary specifications with the cemetery.

☐ **Organize the post-funeral gathering, if you choose to have one.** Often a celebration of the loved one occurs during a luncheon after the funeral. It can be held at a church, mosque, synagogue, private home, banquet hall, or restaurant of your choice. It is a time for fellowship and for the grieving family to be together and greet guests who attended the funeral. Keep in mind, you do not have to do everything—ask friends and relatives to help you set up the luncheon after the funeral.

☐ **Share the ethical will, if there is one.** This is not a legal document, but rather a message to friends and family that shares the loved one's values, life lessons, and hopes for the future. If the deceased wrote one, you should convene his or her loved ones and arrange to have it read aloud.

☐ **Make sure someone is at the home at the time of the funeral or memorial service.** Both online and newspaper obituaries may share the service details. Thieves often target homes of the recently deceased, and are likely to choose the very hour of the ceremony to break in.

☐ **Connect with family and friends of the deceased to share details of the service.** People lead busy lives and some may not readily learn of your loved one's passing. Ask people to contact others who would want to know the details of the funeral arrangements so they will have the information in case they want to participate. You can find important people through the decedent's phone, physical address book, or email account. You can also post the details on social media.

> ### Ask for Help
>
> Identify someone (or a group of people) who can help you write thank-you notes in appreciation of people who sent flowers, delivered food, made a memorial contribution, or assisted you in a special way. Keeping track of all the thank-you messages that need to be sent can be overwhelming, so be sure to set up a tracking system to make this task easier and to ensure no one is overlooked.

In the Days Following a Loved One's Passing

Typically, the funeral or memorial service happens soon after the death of a loved one. The next major step is settling the estate.

Settling the estate means safeguarding the loved one's property during the administration process, paying all debts and taxes, and distributing the assets of the estate to those who are entitled to receive them.

If you are leading this effort, one of your major responsibilities is to be sensitive to the emotional needs of those who are still grieving. Bear in mind that people process the death of a loved one in different ways. Give people time and space to grieve and process the loss. Do not pressure people for decisions or actions when they may be emotionally stressed. Be as sensitive and patient as you possibly can.

Settling the estate is a process, not an overnight event. It is best taken on one step at a time.

☐ **Locate important documents and determine whether any are missing.** Specifically, find out whether there is a will, and confirm that it is the most recent will the deceased signed. This is critical. You should locate all legal documents including trust agreements, any recent bank account statements, and the loved one's Social Security information, as well as relevant documents such as investment statements, tax returns, deeds, birth certificate, marriage certificate, divorce decree (if any), certificates of title to vehicles and property, and details about life insurance policies (a complete list appears below). Keep all these documents in a safe place that more than one person knows about.

About Safety Deposit Boxes and Safes

Many people keep important documents in a safety deposit box at a bank or a safe located in their home. If you do not have a key or combination to open the home safe, enlist help to try to locate the key in your loved one's home and check with family members who may have been given the key or combination for safekeeping. If you are unable to do this, you will have to hire someone to open the safe. The bank will not give you a key without proof of authority and you will have to speak with the bank about its requirements and process.

In addition to the deceased's most recent will, you will want to locate as many of the following items and records as possible:

- ☐ Life insurance policies (obtain all relevant information on premium payments as well)

- ☐ Accidental life insurance

- ☐ Veterans' insurance

- ☐ Mortgage and/or credit insurance

- ☐ Credit card insurance

- ☐ Health insurance (including Medicare or Medicaid, Medigap insurance, private health insurance, dental, and long-term care insurance)

- ☐ Property insurance

- ☐ Employers or pension insurance

- ☐ Workers' compensation insurance (and the related payment records)

- ☐ Deeds, titles, and promissory notes/loans

- ☐ Real estate property deeds, including recent appraisals

- ☐ Mortgage documents, including promissory/loan notes

- ☐ Other promissory/loan notes, including loans owed to the deceased

- ☐ Vehicle titles and registrations

- ☐ Documentation on financial accounts (most recent statements for all these accounts and list of beneficiaries, if available)

- ☐ Bank accounts (checking, savings, CDs, etc.)

- ☐ Investment/brokerage accounts (IRAs, 401(k)s, etc.)

- ☐ Stocks and bonds

- ☐ Annuities

- ☐ Credit and debit card accounts

- ☐ Usernames and passwords for any online accounts

- ☐ List of safety deposit boxes, where to find keys, and names of authorized users

- ☐ Income statements for the current year including Social Security, pension, IRAs, annuities, employment, and other income records

- ☐ Survivor annuity benefit documentation

- ☐ Employer/retirement benefit (pension) plans, pension/profit-sharing plans, etc.

- ☐ Veterans' benefit records

- ☐ Disability payment documents

- ☐ Federal income tax returns (current and previous year)

- ☐ Federal gift tax returns (if any, for all years)

- ☐ Property tax records and statements

- ☐ Business interests held, financial statements and agreements, contracts, etc.

- ☐ Loan documents

- ☐ Passwords to access computers, cell phones, and other electronic devices

- ☐ Other important records

Note that tracking down paperwork and gathering passwords and other essential information can be difficult, time-consuming, and frustrating. You will likely need help. Before you delegate these tasks to an attorney or an accountant who will charge for their services, you may want to consider asking family members for help in gathering the information you need.

Organizing Your Team and Identifying Responsibilities

An important early step is to hold a planning meeting that will help you identify who will be assisting you with specific tasks to help settle the estate.

You may have done some of this work during the funeral planning, but it is important to follow though now to confirm that you know which specific individuals will be taking on which responsibilities. It is also important to confirm that the person or persons acting have the proper authority and experiences.

- ☐ **Review the "Your People" worksheet.** It is likely that *one* person from the worksheet that appears on page 18 of this book should take on the key coordinating role for settling the estate. Determining who that person is (not necessarily the executor) should be the focus of this planning meeting.

Begin by connecting specific names to each of the listed roles, as appropriate, but note that, depending on the complexity of the estate, not all these roles may be relevant.

As you review the "Your People" worksheet, bear in mind that the most time-consuming part of the estate settlement process is typically finding all the documents and compiling an inventory of assets. You will also want to assemble the right group of professionals to assist in settling the estate. That group would consist of the following people:

Legal counsel: The deceased's attorney. This person will likely have copies of the most recent legal documents created, specifically the will. You may eventually opt to hire an attorney specifically for the estate, who may or may not be the deceased's attorney.

Executor: The person who is legally responsible for carrying out the deceased's wishes as outlined in the will and, ultimately, responsible for settling the estate.

Trustee: An individual given control or powers of administration of property in trust, with the legal obligation to administer that property only for the purposes specified in the trust.

Guardian: The legal guardian of minor children previously cared for by the deceased.

Accountant/CPA: The individual who managed the deceased's accounts and/or tax filings. At a later point, you may also opt to hire a CPA with estate experience who can help you to access the estate and identify any potential tax liability before the distribution of assets.

Family contact: The person who knows how best to contact and/or update various family members.

Doctor: It is important to at least have access to the deceased's primary physician so you can access the deceased's medical records if needed.

Financial advisor: The person who helped set up the deceased's long-term financial plan, including investment accounts, life insurance, and any other insurance policies.

Investment advisor: The person who assisted the deceased with their investments.

Insurance professional: The person who helped set up the deceased's insurance policies.

Deceased's employer: The HR or benefits person at the deceased's place of employment.

Realtor: A professional who can help you evaluate and sell real estate. This may or may not be a realtor who worked with the deceased.

Banker: The main person who served as the deceased's liaison with his or her primary bank.

Appraiser for real estate: A professional who can provide date of death value of real property for the estate.

Appraiser for personal assets: A professional who can help you to establish the likely value of specific assets such as collectibles and furniture that belonged to the deceased.

Key support people: Friends and family members who can serve as "document detectives," write thank-you notes, clean out closets, manage inventory, and handle similar roles.

Different Situations, Different Levels of Discovery

No matter how organized the deceased was, there will be a certain amount of "discovery work" that must be completed. You may have to locate accounts and/or even the legal documents you feel the deceased may have prepared. Not surprisingly, there are times when documents were not prepared and accounts were not titled as the deceased may have intended. Start with what you do have. The way an estate can be settled depends, first and foremost, on the legal documents the deceased actually prepared!

The most important of those documents, of course, is the will. Another critical document is a trust. Both are important parts in the discussion about probate.

Wills, Probate, and Trusts

You have probably heard the word "probate" before, but you may be unclear about precisely what that word means. The granting of probate is typically the first step in the legal process of administering the estate of a person who has died. Probate is meant to resolve all outstanding claims against the estate and ensure the proper distribution of the deceased person's property by means of a will. A typical probate period lasts from six months to a year. Probate is public process, and you can potentially face attorney fees, executor commissions, and court costs.

If the deceased had a will and trust (with all assets titled to the trust), it is entirely possible that the estate can avoid probate.

If there is no trust but there is a will that selects the guardians of minor children and selects the executor of the estate, it will give explicit guidance on how the assets of the estate should be distributed.

When someone dies without leaving a will, that person is said to have died "intestate." When that happens the intestacy laws of the state where the deceased resided will determine how their property is distributed. This includes any bank accounts, securities, real estate, and any assets owned at the time of their death. Each state has very specific order of distribution of assets when someone dies without a will.

The Executor

If you are considering taking on the role of executor of the deceased's will, it is important that you first take some time to understand the legal and ethical responsibilities associated with this role.

As executor, you must follow all applicable laws and act in the best interests of the person who has passed away. Your number one responsibility is protecting the estate. Fulfilling this responsibility may require acting against your own interests, and/or acting against the interests of friends or family members. An executor has a *fiduciary responsibility*.

The Executor's Role as a Fiduciary

The word "fiduciary" means "relating to the formal responsibility to take care of someone else's money or property in a suitable way."

If you are unable to accept this responsibility, you should not be in this role.

If you wish to renounce the role of executor and have someone else assume the duties, you should do that early. You can step down as the executor without offering a reason by filing a signed renunciation in probate court after the loved one's death but before the court formally appoints you as executor. The renunciation is a legal document that states that the person named in the will as executor will not act as executor for the estate. Specific rules relating to renunciation will vary based on your situation and where you live. Be sure to notify the estate heirs and will beneficiaries before you submit your renunciation to the court. They will need time to find someone else to act as executor, or to notify the individual named in the will as your successor executor. Important: Although you can petition the court to remove you as executor after you are formally named, it is preferable to disengage from the responsibility of being executor *before* the court formally appoints you. Stepping down after you have formally accepted the court's appointment could leave you open to legal liability from disgruntled heirs and beneficiaries later.

If you do accept the responsibility of serving as executor, you should be aware that if you manage the estate improperly (for instance, by distributing assets before settling with creditors and paying taxes) you could be held personally liable for the monies owed.

Understand that settling the estate will take a while. While the probate process usually takes six months to a year, it can take longer if the executor delays his or her duties or if the estate is complicated. Understand, too, that estate distribution rules will vary by the size of the estate and the state where the property is located.

Learn from the Experience of Others!

Based on common mistakes we have seen executors make, we offer the following suggestions for navigating the demanding tasks of settling the estate:

- ☐ **Do not go it alone.** Trying to do everything yourself when you know the estate is too complex for you to manage without the help of professionals is a huge error. Of course, every estate is different, and you must consider your own situation based on a realistic assessment of what you are facing. For instance, if you have avoided hiring an attorney to save money but you now realize that the estate has issues you cannot address on your own, you should probably call a meeting of your inner circle and discuss the possibility of working with an attorney.

Reality Check

Anna was named the executor of her parents' estate. She was committed to doing the best job she possibly could, and she resolved to safeguard the estate's assets by doing as much of the work herself to avoid paying any more than was necessary for professional help. Instead of hiring a CPA, she chose to handle all the accounting and tax matters on her own. Unfortunately, this approach backfired. She not only raised her own stress and fatigue levels to heights she had never experienced, but she also incurred several expensive penalties from the IRS for late filings and incomplete information.

The lesson: Be prudent with your decisions and consider the possibility that trying to save money by not hiring professional advisors may end up being a costly mistake, both financially and emotionally.

☐ **Do not wait too long to begin the probate process.** It is easy to feel overwhelmed by all the events following the death of a loved one, and it is easy to postpone essential next steps when you feel you still need time to grieve. Even so, there comes a time for action, a time when postponing matters indefinitely will only make the mourning process more stressful and difficult. Discuss timing with your key people, set a realistic schedule for the entire process of settling the estate, and do your best to stick to it.

☐ **Do not put off confirming the actual tax obligations.** There are plenty of sad stories about loved ones who defer tax obligations (such as real estate taxes) for one or more years, without sharing their decisions with family members. When the loved one passes, people assume that there are no encumbrances on the family home and begin settling the estate accordingly—until someone finds out that obligations do exist, and the tax bill must be paid. Regardless of whether you think this kind of thing has happened, you should check with municipal, state, and federal tax authorities on the actual status of the estate's tax obligations *before* you make any disbursements to heirs.

☐ **Remember to maintain good lines of communication with the heirs.** It is essential that you keep in touch with them and let them know how the process is going, what obstacles (if any) you have encountered, and how much progress you have made toward achieving the overriding goal on which you all agreed at the beginning of this process, namely settling the estate in a way that makes sense and honors the wishes of the decedent. We recommend biweekly updates if possible.

☐ **Do not underestimate the importance of closing the estate properly.** Failing to cross all the T's and dot all the I's is all too easy if you have never been an executor before. Unfortunately, end-game mistakes that leave key tasks incomplete can leave you open to significant personal liability.

Avoid Critical Errors as You Close the Estate

"Executors who have properly distributed most of the estate may get tripped up at the very end by failing to properly close the estate. This could vary greatly by the size of the estate, and whether it is administered through the courts or not. Some common ways estates are closed are: (1) filing a family settlement agreement (a.k.a. 'receipt release and indemnification agreement') with the court showing that all beneficiaries are in agreement that they received their share of the estate, or (2) going through a court accounting process where a judge ultimately approves of the distributions. In addition, it is recommended to work with a CPA to ensure all tax matters are closed out or accounted for before the estate is finished with administration." - *Insightlaw.net*

In general, as the executor, you will want to be sure that you do the following:

- ☐ **Secure all the assets right away.** Identify all the tangible assets; quickly change all the locks on all real estate property. Arrange for proper security of all real estate. Remember, it is your responsibility to keep all assets safe until they can be distributed or sold legally and in an organized manner.

- ☐ **Keep the decedent's family informed about your decisions.** The responsibility of the executor is to determine how best to manage the estate settlement, and there are dozens of decisions you will be called upon to make as you do this. Regardless of whether you manage the process alone or rely on professional advisors, it is essential to keep the family informed about what you are planning to do and why. If a decision will potentially affect someone, you should consult that person before you finalize the decision.

- ☐ **Keep thorough records.** Depending on your system for organization, this may mean printing out paper copies of everything and keeping them in a physical binder or file cabinet. Understand that you must have a good filing system because you may be asked to provide documentation of the transactions that happened days, months, or even years later. Some people are not naturally organized. If you are one of those people, you will want to create an alliance with someone who can help you keep track of the mountains of paperwork that you will be expected to handle responsibly.

Caring for Your Loved One's Pets

It is extremely important to honor your loved one's wishes in all regards, especially wishes relating to pet guardianship. Consider the following true story.

Barbara never married and had no children, but she loved her cats with all her heart. When she passed away, she left specific instructions in her will for the person who would take care of her cat, Miss Chips. Her will stated that her neighbor would receive the sum of $1,000 "if he took care of Miss Chips." The neighbor "took care" of the cat by euthanizing it at a local animal shelter. This was obviously not what Barbara wanted, and as a result, the estate filed a declaratory judgment action with the court against the neighbor. The judge ruled that the neighbor's concept of "taking care of the cat" was inconsistent with the intent of the decedent, and he was not given the $1,000.

- ☐ **Be fair and objective.** In the role of executor, you need to be objective, open, and transparent. Avoid favoritism and do not create special opportunities that can be challenged by other beneficiaries of the estate. Create a positive open and honest relationship with your professional advisors and avoid any personal conflict with named beneficiaries.

- ☐ **Do not provide estimates about what people may receive as bequests.** Even well-intentioned guesswork can have major negative effects. There are likely to be too many moving parts for you to be able to make any forecasts about the final distribution.

☐ **Get advice from your inner circle before making any disbursement.** Specifically, do not pay bills too quickly. Consult with your estate attorney to determine which bills need to be paid immediately, which bills can wait, and which bills you will not have to pay. Also, be sure to clarify who is actually the responsible party for paying the bills.

☐ **Do not be too quick to renovate or sell real estate.** Automatically agreeing to home renovations or selling the home is a classic mistake. A family member may suggest this for his or her own reasons. You must determine what is in the best interests of the estate, not any one individual.

☐ **Tactfully decline any attempts to make early disbursements.** Succumbing to pressure to make disbursements too early is another classic mistake. Basic estate expenses must first be covered, and debts must be paid. This is what probate is all about. Making early distributions can leave the estate *and you* open to major legal problems. Specifically, *do not* give away any personal property within the home, even if people make emotional appeals to you to do so. Arrange for an independent appraiser to come in and assess the value of the decedent's personal property before giving away anything.

☐ **Discuss all the tax issues in depth with your attorney and your CPA.** Begin this discussion early in the process. The main reason you must identify *all* the estate's tangible assets is so that you can have a proper inventory list with all the appropriate appraisals.

☐ **Get a tax ID number for the estate and/or trust in order to file your form 1041, also known as a fiduciary tax return. The IRS requires that you file an income tax return for trusts and estates.** The tax ID number for the estate and or trust(s) will also be necessary for you to file returns for state estate taxes and for the deceased's final income tax return. For more information on getting this number, contact the IRS or ask your accountant or attorney.

Officially Becoming the Executor

Once you have accepted the role of executor, you must do the following:

☐ **Obtain, secure, and read the deceased's will.** This may mean doing some detective work to ensure that you have the most recent version of the will.

☐ **File the will** with the local probate court.

☐ **Be officially named** as the executor by the local probate court.

☐ **Determine what kind of probate is necessary, or whether probate is necessary at all.** Probate is a legal process that confirms that the will of a deceased person is valid and that their property can be transferred to beneficiaries of the will. State inheritance laws may allow for the transmission of certain properties without probate (for instance, property held jointly by a husband and wife). A qualified attorney may advise you that probate is not necessary, or that an expedited probate process can be pursued.

☐ **Be ready to represent the estate in court** if necessary.

In addition to taking these initial legal steps, you should be prepared to fulfill the following important responsibilities:

☐ **Attend to permanent dependent arrangements.** Note whether a surviving spouse or child is receiving benefits (Social Security or pension). It can take up to two months after filing for beneficiaries to receive payments, so act as quickly as possible. In addition, make sure any necessary pet care has been arranged for.

☐ **Safeguard all the deceased's valuables.** This means, among other things, making sure there is adequate insurance to protect property in the event of fire, theft, or some other unforeseen event.

☐ **Secure a storage facility if necessary.** If you do decide to go this route, ask for help in moving the deceased's possessions into storage.

☐ **Visit the home, secure it, and collect any mail and newspapers.** This is extremely important, because stacks of uncollected mail and/or newspapers serve as a flashing "rob me" light to criminals that the home is unoccupied. Cancel newspaper deliveries and arrange for mail to be forwarded. Visit the house regularly. On your first visit, discard food and ensure that everything is locked down and appropriate measures are taken to secure the home. You may want to consider changing the locks. Remember, you are responsible for making sure the property is secured and maintained until it transitions to a beneficiary or is sold for cash to be distributed or to pay down the estate's obligations. Bear in mind that unattended or uncollected mail can give unscrupulous people an easy path to commit burglary, identity theft, and other crimes.

☐ **Keep the utilities on at the loved one's home.** You will be using this space to conduct an inventory and perform other essential tasks, and that means essential services should be maintained. If you can, set up an automatic timer for the lights. Save all your receipts and create a spreadsheet documenting all expenses that will need to be reimbursed to keep the home operating as if someone still lived there.

☐ **Remember that it is your duty to oversee and protect *all* the estate's property until it can be distributed or sold.** This point bears repeating. As executor, you must locate all the estate's property and keep it safe until you decide what should be done with it. For instance, do not allow anyone to drive the deceased's automobile. Notify the insurance company providing coverage on any property—including cars, boats, motorcycles, and other valuables— of the deceased's passing. This protects the estate from any unnecessary liability exposure. Remember that you will have to provide the court with a detailed inventory of all the estate's assets.

☐ **Notify creditors in accordance with state law and pay the estate's debts and taxes.** Large estates may have state and/or federal estate taxes to resolve as well.

☐ **Check for unclaimed assets that the decedent owns.** Contact your local secretary of state's office for information on how to access your state's list of unclaimed assets. The estate may have more money at its disposal than you or your loved one realized. The best way to check for unclaimed assets is to visit the MissingMoney.com website.

☐ **Place a small advertisement in the local paper announcing the passing of the decedent and the establishment of the estate.** This is an important precautionary step. Unless the appointment of an executor and the existence of the estate is advertised publicly, creditors may claim that they were never notified and make a claim against the estate. Work with your attorney to make sure you have the right language for this advertisement and that it is placed in an appropriate publication.

Bank Accounts and Bills

Muriel was the executor of her mother's estate. Once a week, she gathered all the incoming mail from her mother's house and swept it into a big cardboard box that she had marked TO BE FILED. The box went unexamined for months. Unfortunately, one of the pieces of correspondence Muriel ignored was a notice from the insurance company informing her mother that her coverage was about to be cancelled due to three months' worth of unpaid premiums! As (bad) luck would have it, her mother's home—the primary asset of the estate—was burgled, and many valuable items were stolen. There was no way to file a claim for the stolen items because there was no policy in place!

To avoid a disastrous situation like that, be sure you take the following steps:

☐ **Set up a bank account for any incoming funds (such as final employment paychecks, tax refunds, etc.) and use this account to pay legitimate bills (such as household expenses and professional service fees).** In addition, note that utilities, mortgages, and other legitimate obligations should now be paid from this estate account. If you had a joint account with the deceased or were a co-signer on that account, you can use those funds if necessary to pay the deceased's regular bills such as property taxes, rental or mortgage payments, credit card bills, and utility bills. Just be sure to keep complete records of all your payments and withdrawals. If you did not have a joint account with the deceased and were not a co-signer, you will need to ask the court to approve you (or someone else) as a personal representative of the deceased who can access the account to pay regular bills. Save and file all your receipts!

☐ **Shut down or memorialize the loved one's social media accounts.**

o Facebook, Google, Instagram, Snapchat, LinkedIn, dating profiles, WhatsApp, Twitter, Venmo – For a complete list, please review the "Digital Asset Inventory" worksheet on page 31.

☐ **Cancel any magazine subscriptions, gym memberships, online accounts, bank accounts, media and phone services, and other memberships in organizations the deceased belonged to.** Keep a written list of the accounts you have shut down.

o **Before closing out credit card accounts or memberships, check whether there are points or credits available for transfer after the deceased's death.**

Negotiate What You Can

Shortly after Dan's passing, his wife, Marie, learned that he had accumulated a significant amount of points on his American Express card. As with most credit cards, the points were nontransferable. Nevertheless, Marie contacted American Express, and after a fair amount of negotiation, she was able to redeem his points for gift cards. She, in turn, gave the gift cards to their nieces and nephews so that they could fly to a family celebration honoring Dan's life. Do not be afraid to ask and to negotiate!

☐ **Notify the post office that the loved one has passed away.** Arrange for mail to be forwarded.

☐ **Request a credit report.** This is an important step to carry out quickly, for two reasons. First and foremost, a credit report can assist in identifying all the active and legitimate credit card and other accounts so that you can compile a complete list of creditors for the estate. Second, you will want to identify any unauthorized purchases that occurred after the loved one's passing. You can obtain a copy of the deceased's credit report by contacting one of the major credit reporting bureaus. Send a request in writing, along with a copy of the death certificate and proof that you are authorized to act on the deceased's behalf, such as a copy of a legal document with a court seal indicating you are the executor of the estate. Here is the contact information for the three largest credit reporting bureaus:

- Experian, 888-397-3742, P.O. Box 9701, Allen, TX 75013

- Equifax, 800-525-6285, P.O. Box 105069, Atlanta, GA 30348

- TransUnion, 800-680-7289, P.O. Box 6790, Fullerton, CA 92834

☐ **Request a death alert.** This is similar to a freeze, which prevents anyone from getting a new credit card, loan or mortgage because lenders and other companies cannot view the credit. Unlike a freeze, which can be lifted, it cannot be undone.

People to Notify

The following steps are extremely important. Don't skip them!

☐ **Alert government agencies, banks, and credit card companies of the person's passing.** It is particularly essential that you inform the Social Security Administration, because doing so will alert the federal government to the passing and it can also deter potential fraudulent claims for the deceased's tax refund (which, unfortunately, is a very common occurrence). Reporting a loved one's death to the Social Security Administration is a straightforward process. Just call 1-800-772-1213 (TTY 1-800-325-0778). You can speak to a Social Security representative between 7 a.m. and 7 p.m. Monday through Friday.

Notify These Offices of the Loved One's Death As Soon As Possible

Social Security Administration, 800-772-1213

US Department of Veterans Affairs (if decedent was formerly in the military), 1-800-827-1000

Defense Finance and Accounting Service (if the decedent was a military service retiree receiving benefits), 800-269-5170

Office of Personnel Management (if the decedent was a retired or former federal civil service employee), 888-767-6738

US Citizenship and Immigration Services (if the decedent was not a U.S. citizen), 800-375-5283

State Department of Motor Vehicles (if the decedent had a driver's license or state ID)

Credit card and merchant card companies

Banks, savings and loan associations, and credit unions

Mortgage companies and lenders

Pension providers

Life insurers and annuity companies

Health, medical, and dental insurers

Disability insurers

Automotive insurers

☐ **Find out whether the surviving spouse or child is eligible to receive Social Security or pension benefits, and make sure the appropriate forms are filed.** It can take beneficiaries up to two months after filing to receive benefits, so be sure to do this as quickly as possible. This step may require consultation over a period of days with family members and/or social service agencies. If the loved one was a current or former member of the armed services, the dependent survivors will want to reach out to the Office of Survivors Assistance, a branch of the US Department of Veterans Affairs (https://www.va.gov/survivors/). If the loved one was eligible for Social Security benefits, his or her spouse, dependent children, or parents may also be eligible. Details are available at https://www.ssa.gov/planners/survivors/ifyou.html. Note that the estate can pay for legitimate expenses related to care of dependents. Again, keep good records and save all your receipts.

☐ **Contact the loved one's employer and/or pension administrator.** If the loved one was working or received pension or health insurance benefits, you will want to get all the details about these arrangements, inform the appropriate parties of the loved one's death, and get the details of any final paycheck that is due. (This final paycheck should go into a new bank account that you set up for the estate.) Depending on state law, the deceased's employer may be legally required to pay back wages to the estate, and to compensate the estate for unused leave, so be sure to ask about this. Find out whether the employer provided a life insurance policy to the loved one. If the answer is yes, ask the employer to provide you with a completed IRS Form 712 and to identify the beneficiaries of the policy.

☐ **Contact the benefit providers.** File for any valid outstanding medical or disability claims on behalf of the estate, and discontinue direct benefit payments to the deceased. If the death resulted from a work-related injury, contact the deceased's workers' compensation insurance provider and discuss the procedure for filing a claim on behalf of the estate.

☐ **Help the spouse of the deceased file for any relevant insurance benefits.** This may include health insurance and supplemental life insurance, depending on the situation. A federal law known as the Consolidated Omnibus Budget Reconciliation Act (COBRA) allows the dependents of employees who have died to maintain the same healthcare coverage that was in place before the person's death by paying the full cost of the premium the employer and the employee previously paid, plus administrative charges.

Prompt action is important in these cases. A dependent spouse must notify the health plan administrator within 30 days of the covered employee's death and may be able to expand coverage up to 36 months.

Death Claims, Retitling Assets, and Related Issues

When Alice's mother died, she left Alice a significant sum of money in a 401(k) account. Alice didn't touch the money; she decided to just let the account sit for a while. Four years later, there was a family emergency, and Alice needed access to the funds. She went to her accountant, Mel, showed him the paperwork, and asked about the best way to withdraw the money she needed. A worried expression passed over Mel's face. "You missed a step," Mel said. "Two years ago, you were supposed to transfer these funds into an IRA beneficiary-designated account, and you were supposed to take a withdrawal. I wish you had shown this to me when you first inherited the asset. Now you're going to have to pay a steep penalty to the IRS!"

Mel was right—the penalty was indeed steep. Alice ended up losing half the money her mother had left her! To avoid similar problems, be sure to complete the following to-do items:

- ☐ **Ask a qualified professional such as an attorney whether assets need to be retitled.** Assets that may need retitling following a person's death include life insurance policies, annuities, retirement accounts, investments, savings accounts, and real estate property. Joint property, such as real estate titled in joint tenancy with the right of survivorship or jointly held bank accounts, transfer automatically to the survivor upon death of either joint owner. All the survivor must do is file a claim. Beneficiary titling on accounts such as life insurance or investments accounts bypass probate; the beneficiary simply submits the claims paperwork. Note that if there are accounts without beneficiaries, the beneficiary is the decedent's estate and the payments will have to be counted as an asset that passes through probate. Beneficiaries may opt not to cash out, but rather to take over ownership of the account. Talk to your financial advisor before you make any decisions.

Distributing Assets

Brian, the executor of his mother's estate, thought his brother Mike's request to take their mom's collection of 1940s-era Walt Disney memorabilia was for sentimental reasons. After all, Mike and his mom had spent decades painstakingly assembling the collection, and their shared passion for early Disney pieces was an important part of their relationship. The day after the funeral, Brian agreed that Mike could take possession of the collection, of which their mom had been sole legal owner. He assumed Mike would eventually hand the collection down to his children. A few months later, Brian was shocked to learn that Mike had sold the individual elements of the collection on eBay and had received over $100,000 from the sales. Brian was even more shocked to learn that, due to several years of missed deadlines and bad planning on the part of their mother's accountant, her estate still owed about $90,000 in back taxes—money that the estate simply did not have, and that Mike didn't have either, because he had used the proceeds from the memorabilia sale to buy a new home.

Brian made a huge mistake by distributing that asset before the estate's financial picture was clear. To avoid a similar mistake, be sure you complete the following to-do items:

- ☐ **Confirm through the court that you have paid the estate's debts (including taxes).** Only when you have done this can you move on the next stage. *Do not* distribute assets attributable to the estate before you are sure that you have paid all the estate's debts. Ask the court whether it will give you a confirmation that all debts and taxes are paid. If you do not get confirmation, find out what obligations remain and determine how they will be resolved."

- ☐ **Distribute the assets to the heirs** based on the wishes of the deceased as set out in the will. A side note is in order here. In order to fulfill your obligations as executor, you will likely need both administrative and diplomatic skills. You are likely to encounter strong personalities and conflicting agendas along the way. Be prepared for this. It may be worthwhile from time to time to remind yourself of the wise words of President Ronald Reagan: "Peace is never the absence of conflict; it is the ability to handle conflict by peaceful means."

☐ **Be prepared to distribute any items the decedent identified in a memorandum of wishes.** This is a simple document that assigns possession of small-financial-value items the deceased chose not to include in the will. It is appropriate for objects that hold primarily sentimental value, such as a ring that is considered a family heirloom, or a sports trophy won in college. Check with your attorney on when it is appropriate to distribute these items.

Identity Theft

Lynne and Max dreamed of the day they would retire together. They had been married for over three decades and were blessed with two adult children who loved them dearly. Lynne worked part time and Max worked full time, commuting daily with his daughter, who also worked in the city. Max liked his job and loved his co-workers. In short, their family lived simply and with great happiness.

Their dreams were shattered when Max suffered a massive stroke and passed away 10 days later without regaining consciousness.

Lynne and Max had planned ahead. Max was taken off life support without incident or controversy because Lynne had access to all the documentation medical staff needed to see. Max had made his final wishes known to his wife, and both the funeral planning and the service went off seamlessly. The family's financial future was secure because, even though they were not wealthy people, Lynne and Max had made sure the right life insurance coverage was in place. Lynne had no financial worries. Everything they owned was titled correctly and the estate was processed seamlessly.

Shortly after the funeral, Lynne received a call from Bank of America. Someone had opened a credit card in Max's name. The news got worse the next day. A little more digging revealed that the person pretending to be Max had actually opened up *four* credit cards! This heartless criminal had also called the post office and forwarded Max's mail to another address. It took a significant investment of time and effort for Lynne to straighten everything out.

We share this story with you because we want you to be prepared. Identify theft is currently the single fastest-growing category of white-collar crime, and deceased people and their families are an easy target.

It is easy for identity thieves to steal the identity of a recently deceased person. According to Die$mart, approximately 400,000 checking accounts are opened annually in the United States using a dead person's name.

Why is it so easy for a dead person's identity to be stolen? Consider the following:

- The published obituary has their name, date of birth, and town they reside in.

- The documents filed in probate court are public information.

- The US Passport Office has no method to be notified that someone has died.

- State driver's license bureaus have no method to receive notice that someone has died.

- Ninety days after death, the decedent's death and name become public information. The Social Security death index provides a record of all deaths, and these records are available on many genealogy websites.

A family member or friend should take immediate action to prevent identity theft of a loved one. Make sure to take the steps to notify credit bureaus and important financial institutions.

The following advice for preventing and dealing with cases of identity theft comes from the Internal Revenue Service (IRS). We have had ample personal experience in helping our clients deal with complex identity theft cases while they were still emotionally processing the death of a loved one.

What is tax-related identity theft? Tax-related identity theft occurs when someone steals your Social Security number (SSN) and uses it to file a tax return to claim a fraudulent refund. You may be unaware that this has happened until you file your return and discover that a return has already been filed using your SSN. Or, the IRS may send you a letter saying it has identified a suspicious return using your SSN.

Know the warning signs

Be alert to possible tax-related identity theft if you are contacted by the IRS or your tax professional/provider about any of the following scenarios:

- More than one tax return was filed using your SSN.

- You owe additional tax, refund offset, or have had collection actions taken against you for a year in which you did not file a tax return.

- IRS records indicate you received wages or other income from an employer for whom you did not work.

If you suspect you are a victim of identity theft, continue to pay your taxes and file your tax return, even if you must do so by paper instead of filing electronically.

☐ **Be wary of any requests for money.** Scammers prey on bereaved families. It is easy for family members and loved ones to be harassed and traumatized because of bogus funeral and memorial funds being set up following the online announcement of an individual's death.

Steps to take if you become a victim

If you are a victim of identity theft, the Federal Trade Commission (FTC) recommends these steps:

- ☐ File a complaint with the FTC at identitytheft.gov.

- ☐ Contact one of the three major credit bureaus to place a fraud alert on your credit records.

  - o Equifax, www.Equifax.com, 800-525-6285

  - o Experian, www.Experian.com, 888-397-3742

  - o TransUnion, www.TransUnion.com, 800-680-7289

☐ Contact your financial institutions and close any financial or credit accounts opened without your permission or tampered with by identity thieves.

If your SSN is compromised and you know or suspect you are a victim of tax-related identity theft, the IRS recommends these additional steps:

☐ Respond immediately to any IRS notice; call the number provided.

☐ Complete IRS Form 14039, Identity Theft Affidavit, if your filed return is rejected because of a duplicate filing under your SSN or you are instructed to do so. Use a fillable form at IRS.gov, print it, then attach the form to your return and follow the mailing instructions.

☐ If you previously contacted the IRS but did not achieve a resolution, contact us for specialized assistance at 1-800-908-4490. We have teams available to help.

About data breaches and your taxes

Not all data breaches or computer hacks result in tax-related identity theft. It is important to know what type of personal information was stolen.

If you are the victim of a data breach, keep in touch with the company to learn what it is doing to protect you and follow the steps listed above for victims of identity theft. Submit a Form 14039, Identity Theft Affidavit, only if your Social Security number has been compromised and your filed return was rejected as a duplicate, or the IRS has informed you that you may be a victim of tax-related identity theft.

How can you reduce your risk of your identity being stolen?

• Always use security software with firewall and antivirus protections. Use strong passwords.

• Learn to recognize and avoid phishing emails, threatening calls, and texts from thieves posing as legitimate organizations such as your bank, credit card companies, and even the IRS.

- Do not click on links or download attachments from unknown or suspicious emails.

- Protect your personal information and that of any dependents. Do not routinely carry your Social Security card, and make sure your tax records are secure.

See Publication 4524, Security Awareness for Taxpayers, to learn more.

Beware of IRS impersonation scams

The IRS does not initiate contact with taxpayers by email to request personal or financial information. This includes any type of electronic communication, such as text messages and social media channels. You can report suspicious online or emailed phishing scams to phishing@irs.gov. For phishing scams by phone, fax, or mail, call 1-800-366-4484. Report IRS impersonation scams to the Treasury Inspector General for Tax Administration's IRS Impersonation Scams Reporting by visiting their website www.treasury.gov/tigta/contact_report_scam.shtml.

☐ **File a report.** You can and should report identity theft to the Federal Trade Commission (FTC) online at IdentityTheft.gov or by phone at 1-877-438-4338. If you report identity theft online, the FTC will help you arrange for an identity theft report and a recovery plan. You will be able to create an account on the website that will allow you to update your recovery plan, track your progress, and receive prefilled form letters to send to creditors. If you opt not to create an account, you can still print and save your identity theft report and recovery plan. You can also download the FTC's publication, *Taking Charge: What to Do If Your Identity Is Stolen* for detailed tips, checklists, and sample letters. You may also choose to report your identity theft to your local police station. This will be necessary if you know the identity thief, if the thief used your name in any interaction with the police, or if a creditor or another company affected by the identity theft requires you to provide a police report. Go to www.identifytheft.com for more information.

Closing Thoughts

Take care of yourself! The death of a loved one can take a toll on your health and the health and well-being of your family. Each person will grieve in their own way and at their own pace. Grief has no timetable and affects everyone differently. It is critically important that you take care of yourself and get the support you need, both emotionally and professionally. Find strength and support within your inner circle. Allow yourself ample time to do the things that energize your soul and keep you engaged, healthy, and happy. Be sure to accept help, love, and support to nourish your soul and keep you grounded as you go through this difficult time in your life.

Don't wait to take action! The reason you have worked through this guidebook is to give the ultimate gift to your loved ones—closure the way you want it to happen.

Death will always be an uncomfortable topic, and there are numerous reasons people avoid the subject. It is unsettling to think about your own mortality and depressing to think of loved ones dying. Most often, people feel bad about asking others to manage their affairs at the end of their lives—it is a big commitment. The loss of a loved one is not just a major emotional event, it can also be a major financial event for the survivors. At the end of life, most people simply want comfort, respect, and love from family and friends. Those who are left behind want the time to grieve. Everyone dies eventually, whether expected or not. When you take the time to prepare for death in advance, you relieve your family of the burden of making decisions. Through careful planning your loved ones will be able to grieve and move forward with some structure in executing your wishes, which will make it a little easier to live on without you.

By Taking Action. Life is ever-changing and if you are waiting for the perfect time to put your affairs in order, you will never take the first step. Our desire in writing this guidebook was to share our experiences and encourage you to take action. If you have undertaken the serious and substantial work of settling someone else's estate, you are now, by definition, in possession of some extremely important personal lessons about how to make it easy for someone else to settle yours.

Use this guidebook as a resource to prepare your own affairs for those who will come after you and be responsible for settling your affairs.

We would love to hear your feedback on how this guidebook served you, and on any areas we could improve in a future edition. Please reach out to us at (978) 689-8200.

Worksheets

Your People

Executor

Name _____
Address _____
City/State/Zip _____
Telephone _____
Email _____

Financial Advisor

Name _____
Address _____
City/State/Zip _____
Telephone _____
Email _____

Attorney

Name _____
Address _____
City/State/Zip _____
Telephone _____
Email _____

Insurance Advisor

Name _____
Address _____
City/State/Zip _____
Telephone _____
Email _____

Clergy

Name _____
Address _____
City/State/Zip _____
Telephone _____
Email _____

Physician

Name _____
Address _____
City/State/Zip _____
Telephone _____
Email _____

Pharmacist

Name _____
Address _____
City/State/Zip _____
Telephone _____
Email _____

Durable Power of Attorney

Name _____
Address _____
City/State/Zip _____
Telephone _____
Email _____

Health Care Proxy

Name _____
Address _____
City/State/Zip _____
Telephone _____
Email _____

Accountant

Name _____
Address _____
City/State/Zip _____
Telephone _____
Email _____

Employer

Name _____
Address _____
City/State/Zip _____
Telephone _____
Email _____

Therapist

Name _____
Address _____
City/State/Zip _____
Telephone _____
Email _____

Dentist

Name _____
Address _____
City/State/Zip _____
Telephone _____
Email _____

Other

Name _____
Address _____
City/State/Zip _____
Telephone _____
Email _____

Asset Inventory and Location

For the Estate of _____

Executor's Name:

Date Checklist Completed:

Obtain copies of each of the following items and place in the same envelope as this Document Guide.

Legal Papers

- ❑ Will and/or trusts
- ❑ Letter of specific bequests
- ❑ Ethical will
- ❑ Deceased's final instructions, Disposition authorization, and/or Designated agent forms (sometimes included in an Advance Directive such as a Durable Power of Attorney for Health Care, or in a Living Will)
- ❑ Prepaid funeral contracts (cemetery plot information)
- ❑ Copy of driver's license
- ❑ Organ/tissue donation record
- ❑ Social Security card (or number)
- ❑ Birth certificates (of all family members)
- ❑ Marriage license or certificate
- ❑ Military service papers, including discharge records
- ❑ Domestic partnership registration
- ❑ Court documents for adoptions and divorce (including any property settlement agreements, name changes, prenuptial agreements, etc.)
- ❑ Community property agreements
- ❑ Passport, citizenship, immigration, and/or alien registration papers
- ❑ Pre-marital agreement

Personal Information

- ❑ Names and contact information of closest family and friends
- ❑ Names and contact information of all lawyers, accountants, doctors, etc.
- ❑ Family tree, if available (especially if there is no will)
- ❑ In-home safe (who has key/combination and access to it)

Financial Accounts: Primary and Contingent Beneficiary Designation Forms

- ❑ Bank accounts – checking, savings, CDs, etc.
- ❑ Investment/brokerage accounts, IRAs, 401(k), 403(b), SEP, HSA, FSA, etc.
- ❑ Stocks and bonds
- ❑ Annuities
- ❑ Nonqualified pension plan
- ❑ Credit and debit card accounts
- ❑ List of safety deposit boxes, where to find keys, and names of authorized users

Other Financial Records

- ☐ Survivor annuity benefit papers
- ☐ Employer/retirement benefit (pension) plans, pension/profit-sharing plans, etc.
- ☐ Veterans benefit records
- ☐ Disability payment documents (state, veterans, etc.)
- ☐ Income statements for the current year (Social Security, pension, IRAs, annuities, employment, and other income records)
- ☐ IRS income tax returns (for the current and previous year)
- ☐ IRS gift tax returns (if any, for all years)
- ☐ Property tax records and statements
- ☐ Business interests held, financial statements and agreements, contracts, etc.
- ☐ Loan papers
- ☐ Other (investment records, etc.)

Property, Deeds, Titles, and Promissory Notes/Loans

- ☐ Real estate property deeds (including any recent appraisals)
  - ☐ Primary home
  - ☐ Secondary home
  - ☐ Timeshare
  - ☐ Investment real estate
  - ☐ Commercial real estate
- ☐ Mortgage documents (including promissory/loan notes/discharge paperwork)
- ☐ Other promissory or loan notes (including loans owed to the deceased)
- ☐ Vehicle registrations (car, boat, RV, Jet Ski, etc.)
- ☐ Property leases
- ☐ Community care retirement agreement
- ☐ Storage unit (location and key)
- ☐ Collectibles (stamp collection, war medals, coin collections, etc.)
- ☐ Student loan (s) (protection rider)

Insurance Policies

- ☐ Life insurance
- ☐ Disability insurance
- ☐ Medical and dental insurance
- ☐ Health/dental insurance membership cards
- ☐ Long-term care insurance
- ☐ Homeowner's/rental insurance
- ☐ Auto insurance
- ☐ Umbrella liability insurance
- ☐ Other insurance
- ☐ Asset appraisals (jewelry)
- ☐ Accidental life insurance
- ☐ Veterans insurance

- ❏ Employers or pension insurance
- ❏ Funeral insurance (or other death-related benefit plans)
- ❏ Mortgage and/or credit insurance
- ❏ Credit card insurance (for balances)
- ❏ Workers' compensation insurance (and payment records)

Beneficiary/Owner Checklist

Legal Documents

- ❑ Will
- ❑ Trust

Insurance Policies

- ❑ Life insurance
- ❑ Disability
- ❑ Accidental life insurance
- ❑ Veterans insurance
- ❑ Employers group insurance
- ❑ Retiree group insurance
- ❑ Funeral insurance (or other death-related benefit plans)
- ❑ Mortgage and/or credit insurance
- ❑ Credit card insurance (for balances)
- ❑ Long-term care insurance
- ❑ Workers' compensation insurance (and payment records)

Financial Accounts

- ❑ Bank accounts—checking, savings, CDs, etc.
- ❑ HSA/FSA/dependent care
- ❑ Investment/brokerage accounts, IRAs, 401(k)s, etc.
- ❑ Stocks and bonds
- ❑ Annuities
- ❑ Deferred compensation
- ❑ Cash balance plans
- ❑ Stock option plans
- ❑ Safety deposit box (who is authorized to access)

Digital Asset Inventory

Device	Website	Username	Password
Computer – Home			
Computer – Office			
Cell Phone			
iPad			
iCloud			

Email Accounts	Email Address	Username	Password

Social Networks	Website	Username	Password	Disposition Desires
Facebook				
LinkedIn				
Twitter				
Google				
Instagram				
Snapchat (photo vault)				
Dating Profile/Website				
Digital Subscriptions				
○ Amazon				
○ Airlines				
○ Uber				
○ Lyft				
○ Newspapers				
Other				

Estate Planning Items for Discussion

Providing the following information can help your attorney develop an appropriate estate plan for You and your spouse or significant other.

1. **Who Will Make Financial Decisions?**

   Who will make financial decisions for you and your spouse? List the full names with middle initials, addresses, telephone numbers, and email addresses for your first and second choices.

   1. Name   _____
      Address   _____
      Telephone _____
      City/State/Zip _____
      Email   _____

   2. Name   _____
      Address   _____
      Telephone _____
      City/State/Zip _____
      Email   _____

2. **Who Will Make Medical Decisions?**

   Who will make medical decisions (including possibly end-of-life decisions)? List the full names with middle initials, addresses, telephone numbers, and email addresses for your first and second choices.

   1. **For** _____

      Name   _____
      Address   _____
      City/State/Zip _____
      Telephone _____
      Email   _____

   2. **For** _____

      Name   _____
      Address   _____
      City/State/Zip _____
      Telephone _____
      Email   _____

   1. **For** _____

      Name   _____
      Address   _____
      City/State/Zip _____
      Telephone _____
      Email   _____

   2. **For** _____

      Name   _____
      Address   _____
      City/State/Zip _____
      Telephone _____
      Email   _____

3. **Who Should Inherit Your Property?**

Who will inherit your property? List the percentage of your total estate rather than specific assets. Include the full name and relationship to each party.

Name_____Relationship_____% _____

Name_____Relationship_____% _____

Name_____Relationship_____% _____

4. **If Your Heirs Predecease You**

If any of your heirs predecease you, who should inherit their share of your estate? Name each heir and an alternate.

Heir _____   Alternate _____

Heir _____   Alternate _____

Heir _____   Alternate _____

5. **Caring For Minor Children**

If there are minor children, who will raise them if both parents are deceased? List the full name, address, telephone number, email address, and personal relationship for each guardian. List individuals rather than naming a couple.

Name   _____

Address   _____

City/State/Zip _____

Telephone   _____

Email   _____

Relationship _____

Name   _____

Address   _____

City/State/Zip _____

Telephone   _____

Email   _____

Relationship _____

6. At What Age Should Your Children or Young Adult Heirs Inherit Property?
This age may vary with the individual.

Name _____   Age to Inherit _____

Name _____   Age to Inherit _____

Name _____   Age to Inherit _____

Name _____   Age to Inherit _____

Name _____   Age to Inherit _____

Many people like to distribute a portion of the estate at several different times. For example, 1/3 at age 21, 1/3 at age 25 and 1/3 at age 30; or ½ at age 30 and ½ at age 35, etc.

If you want to influence either the timing of the inheritance or the way it gets spent, you'll need to use a trust.

This worksheet helped you prepare to get your legal documents completed or reviewed and revised. It did not legally bind any decisions. Furthermore, instructions in existing legal documents or newly created legal documents will override anything written here.

Funeral Planning

Planning your own funeral or memorial service can provide priceless peace-of-mind to you and your family.

Your wishes for your body:

- ❑ **Cremation**
  - ❑ Before funeral
  - ❑ After funeral
  - ❑ Disbursement of ashes _____

- ❑ **Burial**

  Type of property
  - ❑ Mausoleum ❑ Ground burial ❑ Lawn crypt ❑ Urn/Niche
  - ❑ Legal description (if known) _____
  - ❑ Type of memorial/marker _____
  - ❑ Is there an inscription/epitaph you would like _____
  - ❑ Mortuary/funeral home/cemetery
    - Name _____
    - Address _____
    - Phone number _____

  Have you prepaid for any funeral services? ❑ Yes ❑ No

  I have the right to be buried in a military cemetery
  ❑ Yes ❑ No

  I have a deceased
  ❑ Spouse ❑ Parent ❑ Child who is buried at _____

  I wish to be buried next to such person _____

Casket Preferences

- ❑ Least expensive ❑ Midrange ❑ Elaborate ❑ I have prepaid

Do you want a "visitation" prior to the funeral service?
❑ Yes ❑ No

Do you want the casket open for viewing?
❑ Yes ❑ No

If yes, by whom?
❑ Family only ❑ Everyone ❑ Selected people only

Donate Your Body or Organs for Medical Study

❑　　No

❑　　Yes, arrangements have been made

❑　　Yes, please make appropriate arrangements

Prayers, Poems, Readings

I would like the following people to deliver prayers or other readings:

1. _____

2. _____

3. _____

The readings I would like them to deliver are _____

Title _____　　Author/Source _____

Songs/Music

I would like the following songs, hymns, or pieces of music to be played:

1. _____

2. _____

3. _____

Flowers/Donations

I would prefer the following types of flowers: _____

Would you like donations in lieu of flowers?

❑　Yes　❑　No

If so, list details here:

Service

What type of service do you want to have?

Location:

I would like my funeral or memorial service to be held at the following location: _____

If this location is not available, my second choice is _____

I have papers on file at: _____

Officiant

I would like the following person to officiate at my funeral or memorial service:_____

If this person is not available, my second choice is: _____

Pallbearers

I would like the following people to serve as pallbearers:
1.
2.
3.
4.
5.
6.

I would like the following people to serve as honorary pallbearers:

1.
2.

Eulogies

I would like the following people to deliver eulogies:

1.

2.

Special Notifications

Are there any groups, organizations, and clubs (veteran's groups, alumni associations, sports or hobby clubs, etc.) you would like to be notified of and invited to your funeral or memorial service?

Name of Group/Primary Contact_____

Contact Information _____

Please be sure the following people are notified of and invited to my funeral or memorial service

Name_____   Contact Information _____

Name_____   Contact Information _____

Name_____   Contact Information _____

Other Special Requests

Are there specific clothes you would like to be buried in or is there specific jewelry you would like to wear?

Military flag given to (if applicable) _____

Obituary

Please publish my obituary
❏ Yes ❏ No

I have already drafted an obituary. ❏ Yes (Location_____) ❏ No

If I have not drafted an obituary, please prepare one using the following information and instructions below.

Obituary Overview
    Length: ❏ Brief ❏ Moderate ❏ Article Length
    Photograph: ❏ Yes (Location_____) ❏ No
    Publications:

Obituary Details
    Date and place of birth
    Military service
    Spouse, children, grandchildren, parents, siblings
    Employment and business interests
    Memberships and committees
    Education
    Awards and achievements
    Interests and hobbies
    Values

Public or Private

My wishes for public or private ceremonies
    ❏ Viewing, visitation, or wake
    ❏ Funeral or memorial service
    ❏ Reception or celebration of life

Flowers
    ❏ Yes
    ❏ No. "No flowers, please."
    ❏ No. In lieu of flowers, please send donations to [list organization(s)].

Lastly, make sure your loved ones know your wishes. Share this worksheet with them and make sure to keep a copy with your other important documents.

ABOUT THE AUTHORS

Jennifer A. Borislow is the founder and Chief Executive Officer of Borislow Insurance, a leading provider of innovative health and well-being benefits solutions. Borislow Insurance serves more than 300 businesses throughout New England with an expertise in transforming workplace culture by creating a community of consumerism and empowering employees to make informed health care choices. With her business partner, Mark S. Gaunya, she is the co-author of four books: *Bend the Healthcare Trend,* which has entered its second edition, *Inspire to Act,* and *Inspire to Act for Kids.* She is an industry leader and active participant on several insurance company advisory boards. Jennifer currently serves as trustee at Northern Essex Community College and is also on the board of trustees of the Merrimack Valley YMCA. She is a frequent keynote speaker at many national and international events. Her commitment to community involvement is highlighted by her passion to make a difference in the lives of others.

For two decades, **Melissa A. Marrama** has been committed to solving problems and helping her clients feel secure in their decisions. Her clients include closely held businesses, individuals, and families at all stages. She advises on issues ranging from accumulating and protecting wealth to how to best enjoy it in retirement. Both inside Borislow Insurance and with clients and friends, Melissa has earned a reputation of sitting on the client's side of the table and going above and beyond to ensure her clients' comprehensive financial well-being. Melissa holds a Bachelor of Science in Finance from Bentley College. She consistently earns member status in two prestigious organizations of insurance executives that set the standards for professionalism, the National Association of Insurance and Financial Advisors and the Million Dollar Round Table. Her genuine desire to help others is evident not only in her professional work but also in her many charitable endeavors and her prominent positions with charitable organizations.

 Making the complex understandable and achievable has driven **Michaela F. Scott's** entire career as a financial services executive. Michaela partners with business owners and individuals who have taken a sincere interest in their financial future and who want to control their legacy so as to benefit their children, their business, a specific charity, or all the above. Her professional accolades consistently highlight her mission—to listen, understand, and help clients identify and thoughtfully address their unique goals and most pressing concerns. Active memberships in professional organizations such as the Million Dollar Round Table and National Association of Estate Planners and Councils keep Michaela current and connected. Michaela takes a team approach, leveraging top talent to uncover opportunity and define clear and implementable solutions. She is a Certified Financial Planner™ who earned her Master of Science in Financial Services with a concentration in Retirement Planning from The American College of Financial Services. Michaela holds an honors Bachelor of Arts in Politics from Saint Anselm College.